Battleground Europe

YPRES

PASSCHENDAELE
The Fight for the Village

D1059024

Battleground Europe

YPRES

PASSCHENDAELE
The Fight for theVillage

Nigel Cave

Series editor
Nigel Cave

LEO COOPER

To my brethren of the English and Welsh Province of the Institute of Charity who have proved to be both tolerant and supportive of my interest in the Great War.

First published in 1997
Reprinted 2000, 2003
LEO COOPER
an imprint of
Pen Sword Books Limited
47 Church Street, Barnsley, South Yorkshire S70 2AS

Copyright © Nigel Cave, 1997, 2000, 2003

ISBN 0 85052 558 6

A CIP catalogue of this book is available
from the British Library

Printed by CPI UK

For up-to-date information on other titles produced under the Leo Cooper imprint, please telephone or write to:

Pen & Sword Books Ltd, FREEPOST, 47 Church Street
Barnsley, South Yorkshire S70 2AS
Telephone 01226 734222

CONTENTS

ACKNOWLEDGEMENTS

As usual in my books on the battlefields, my first and most vital acknowledgement is to the authors of the various regimental, divisional and corps histories who have provided much of the material in this book. Without them visits to the battlefields would be far less meaningful; although their works were often for the benefit of their members during the Great War, they have found a new readership in recent years. One unfortunate consequence is the escalation in their price, if you are lucky enough to find them in the first place!

I am most grateful to Ted Smith for the cover photograph; the painting is his and he also provided me with the transparency.

Ralph Whitehead in the United States has done tremendous work for me by translating various German accounts, sending me photographs and generally doing nearly all the donkey work for me as regards the German view of Passchendaele. He is also doing lots of other work for myself and other authors in this series; without his contribution an important element in the story of the battlefields - ie the perspective of the enemy – would not be covered.

I am also most grateful to the generosity of Norbert Krüger of Essen who has provided me with some wonderful photographs, maps and other useful information. I met Norbert by chance at Delville Wood and his immediate willingness to help and to entrust me with valuable – and unique – material is deeply appreciated.

Assistance from the Commonwealth War Graves Commission has been of its usual impeccable and helpful standard. I would particularly like to thank Beverly Webb, who over the years has never failed to put herself out to help with queries. The loan service for registers has been particularly useful. The cemeteries and memorials in the area described in the book are, as one has come to expect, beautifully looked after and reflect so well on the Commission. The only one that is showing signs of wear is Tyne Cot, and that is because of the extraordinary upsurge of interest in the Great War and the thousands of feet consequent upon this that give the grass in that cemetery such a testing time.

When doing the research for this book I stayed at Talbot House; and indeed on one memorably sunny day in October enjoyed the company of Jacques Ryckebosch and Juan Tetaere from the House as I walked and drove the ground covered in the book. I would also like to thank Mark Fisher who endured some miserable days in January with me around Passchendaele.Others were also willing to have part of their tour with me directed to Passchendaele, and so thanks are due to Professor Brian Bond, Colonel Simon Doughty, my father, Colonel Terry Cave and Dr Graham Keech.

Albert Beke of the Cloth Hall has always been a helpful and welcoming friend, and no visit to Ypres is complete without seeing him and the 1914 - 1918 museum situated in the Cloth Hall. The Tourist Office in Zonnebeke has been most helpful, and I would strongly advise visitors to find the time to visit the impressive museum there.

I am, as ever, grateful to my sparring partner in Barnsley, Roni Wilkinson, who makes the production and design of these books a labour of love; the success of this series owes much to his imagination and vision. The authorities at Ratcliffe College have kindly permitted my removal of a school vehicle on several occasions to tour the battlefields and their generosity has been essential in the preparation of this work. I am particularly grateful to Mrs Pauline Davies at the College, who very kindly came to my rescue and typed out some 'lost' material for me again at very short and inconvenient notice.

This book is dedicated to my brethren in the English and Welsh Province of the Institute of Charity (Rosminians). Over the years they have tolerated my unclerical fascination with the Great War, and more recently have enabled me to have several years to work for a Doctorate in this area. I am deeply grateful.

85th (Nova Scotia) Battalion Canadian Expeditionary Force
I first found this memorial last year – references to it will be found in the index. During the course of my research I became aware that the future of this memorial is under threat.

Firstly I would like to make it clear that this situation has nothing to do with the CWGC who care for it as agents, or the Canadian authorities. It seems that the memorial, as I understand the matter, provides a number of problems. The memorial is some 150 yards along a grass path surrounded by fields. There is no parking facility. The access path, it seems, interferes with the smooth runing of two farms. It is certainly true that the memorial is unmarked; that parking (just about) exisits for only one vehicle and that the path is long. I can well understand that it is inconvenient and, as some people have pointed out with some justification, history should not stand in the way of people's livelihood.

If it is decided that the memorial has to go, the suggestion is that the plaque, which names the thirteen officers and 135 other ranks of the battalion who fell here, should be translated to the Canadian national memorial to the west of Passchendaele at Crest Farm. The rest of the memorial could not survive the transfer.

There are practical grounds for these arguments, I would agree. **However, there are emotional and historic grounds for fighting such a move.** This is the only Canadian battalion memorial on the Western Front that lists the dead in an action; the only one which describes the action; the only one which marks the site of the battle headquarters of the battalion and the only one to be erected before the battalion returned to Canada. There is only one other Canadian battalion memorial on the old Great War battlefields (that of the PPCLI on Bellewaarde Ridge). To move it to Crest Farm would make the battlefield description on the plaque meaningless and quite frankly I think it would be better to take it to Halifax if matters came to that point. Readers who feel strongly about this issue should ensure that the matter does not come about because of an apparent lack of interest, and perhaps they might like to write to me via Pen and Sword so that I can pass their views on to the relevant authorities. I might add that I am most grateful for the help and assistance I have had from various Canadian Parliamentarians, High Commission staff and others who have humoured me. I would like to point out that the Regiment is completely opposed to any proposal to move this memorial. Over 150 men gave their lives from this battalion in the last days of October 1917; so did thousands more from the opposing armies in these fraught, horrific and miserable days of 1917. This simple memorial is an evocation of not just their sacrifice and premature death but of the thousands who died or were wounded in the battle for Passchendaele. They deserve our respect and remembrance – even if it is a little inconvenient.

PASSCHENDAELE: AN INTRODUCTION

The Third Battle of Ypres is known to the public as Passchendaele. This is highly misleading, as the battle that raged around this large Flemish village occupied only the last weeks of a battle that lasted for over three months; and even the fighting of the last weeks was not exclusively concerned with the capture of Passchendaele and the ground immediately around it. The image of this battle has been used as epitomising the battle scene – and to some extent the conduct – of the whole of the Great War, and that, too, is misleading. At one stage in September the complaints about the dust and shortage of water were as vociferous as those about the mud in October. This book is a guide, and therefore tries to avoid being contentious; it is meant to record what happened from the viewpoint of some of those who took part in it.

I have had to be selective about the formations and units that I have written about. To fit all of those involved in the attack on Passchendaele Ridge would have made the book too large, and arguably indigestible, for a visitor to the area, at least in one go. Therefore this book deals exclusively with the attacks launched by the New Zealanders and the Canadian Corps; omitted are the Imperial (British) and Australian troops engaged; they will be the subject of a later book in the series, and their omission in this case is therefore entirely deliberate. Their courage, valour, tenacity and actions will get similar coverage in due course.

There has always been considerable controversy about Haig's decision to continue the battle after the successes of 4 October, the Battle of Broodseinde. I would suggest that after visiting the battlefield, perhaps finding a convenient place to stop near Bellevue or along the Passchendaele – Zonnebeke road, the visitor would see that there was at least a topographical point to the exercise. From Bellevue – and indeed Mosselmarkt to the east of it – the Germans had clear and uninterrupted views across the British lines, to Ypres and beyond. When the British reached the top of the ridge to the south of Passchendaele they deprived the Germans of much of that view (although they did retain high ground around Westrozebeke) and indeed offered the British a commanding vantage point over the German lines to the east. It was certainly a more comfortable, if that is the right word, position in which to spend the winter.

Of course it placed the British in a vulnerable salient, and although it might have acted as a suitable launch pad for a new Allied offensive in the better weather of Spring 1918, it was the Germans who launched their attack here in April, and they rapidly regained all the ground that had been so hard fought for and more; contrariwise the British and Belgians very rapidly regained it in September of that year, and then pushed out of the Salient finally in the early part of October.

There is a, perhaps understandable, tendency to see the great battles of the Western Front in isolation – Loos, the Somme, Passchendaele and so forth. It is worth bearing in mind that the British offensives of 1917 were almost uninterrupted. They commenced in April in the Battle of Arras, notable for being almost completely neglected as an object of historical study with the single exception of Vimy Ridge; in June the highly successful Messines Offensive was launched; at the end of July Third Ypres opened up, with a notable action by the Canadian Corps around Lens, well to the south, taking place during it; as soon as it finished, Cambrai was fought – it was a very busy year for British arms. Whatever the rights and wrongs of decisions made by the generals – and the politicians, for that matter – there is no doubt that the German High Command came to the conclusion by the end of the year that it was no longer possible to fight merely a defensive battle. Battles with big objectives might have become a thing of the past, but the idea that a position could be held against a full artillery programme and determined infantry was no longer tenable, in more ways than one.

This book concentrates, for the most part, on the Canadians. They fought here for a quite short period of time – eleven days in major battles, another two weeks or so afterwards holding the line. In those eleven days they won nine Victoria Crosses – which can be compared with the ten that they won in the whole of the Second World War. This is no reflection on the men of the Second War; rather it is an indication of the heights of heroism, initiative and endurance that the circumstances of this Passchendaele battle demanded for success to be achieved; conditions which are reflected in that name having such a high place in 'modern memory'.

Nigel Cave
Ely Place, London

Passchendaele: Advice to Tourers

It Is probably best to read this book first at home so that you have a reasonable idea of what lies ahead of you. The touring part of the book has walks in it which do try and keep to the boundaries of a limited number of actions so that confusion is not caused; of the four suggested tours two can be done by car and two require some off the road (on good tracks) walking, but even these latter can be done in a car if circumstances (or weather) require it by making only minor adjustments.

The obvious place to stay when visiting this part of Belgium is Ypres (Ieper in Flemish – and the name on most sign posts in this Flemish part of Belgium). At the side of the Cloth Hall, on the Menin Gate side of the building, is the local Tourist Office, which has lists of hotels and Bed and Breakfasts. Ypres is also the place to eat – Passchendaele and area is not over-endowed with cafés and restaurants, and there are numerous square-side cafés in town.

Ypres is a pleasant, atmospheric town today, with a feel of old world charm about the centre. In 1914 it would have been a lot sleepier, but it was still a large market town. The ancient buildings are, of course, all a sham, not least the monumental Cloth Hall itself – lovingly restored from the utter devastation of the Great War. The Rev EV Tanner MC* was the padre to 2/Worcesters in 1917 when he decided to visit the place on Sunday 23 September, and his diary records what the town looked like then

'Being on the direct road to Ypres and only about two kilometres from it, the Doctor and I thought that we would like to pay a visit to what is I suppose the most famous town on the Western front – certainly the scene of the fiercest and most continual fighting. We walked in about 3.30 and really I would not have missed the sight for anything. Picture a large and prosperous town completely reduced to ruins with not a house standing sufficiently to provide shelter. If the Cloth Hall was a wonderful sight before the war it is even more wonderful now. The bare shell still stands and speaks of the former grandeur of the building, the rest is just one big pile of stone and rubbish. While we were sitting down in the Grande Place trying to take in the details of this wonderful sight a squadron of five German aeroplanes flew impudently and at quite a low altitude over the town. It was at once attacked by six or seven of our own planes and a Battle Royal ensued. The air was filled with the rattle of

11

The ruins of the Cloth Hall at Ypres, September 1917.

machine guns and the falling of splinters from the anti-aircraft guns. When this excitement had died away and the intruders had been driven back to their own lines I went through the vaulted archway of the Cloth Hall and wandered over the ruins and into the ruined Cathedral at the back. I found a small stone pinnacle about a foot long amongst the rubbish and should love to take it home as souvenir. Being too heavy to take now I buried it in the Doctor's presence at the foot of the middle column of the main entrance to the ruined Cathedral. Perhaps I shall have an opportunity of getting back to it...'

Whilst in Ypres one should visit the Cloth Hall Museum, though this is due to be extensively refurbished over the winter of 1997-1998. This museum has extended dramatically in size since my first visit in 1968, when it occupied a small chamber in the tower; now it occupies half of the first floor. After the refurbishment, I understand, it will take up the

whole of that floor. At the moment it houses a wide variety of artefacts, models, medals, photographs and various items of military hardware. The new museum may well not be to everyone's taste. Not far from Ypres, about two or three miles away, is the Trench Museum at Sanctuary Wood; a first rate small museum in the old Hooge Chapel and some trench lines by Hooge Crater in the grounds of the Hooge Château Hotel (see my *Sanctuary Wood and Hooge* in this series); there is also a rather disorganised but engaging museum

Tableau of a British trench in the museum at Zonnebeke.

at Hill 60, housed in the Queen Victoria's Rifles Café (see my *Hill 60* in the same series).

St George's Memorial Church is the Anglican Church in Ypres; its walls are covered with plaques commemorating the many British and Dominion Regiments and individuals that served and fought here during the war and is well worth a visit.

No visit to the Salient would be complete without attending the sounding of the Last Post under the Menin Gate at 8 pm each evening; the ceremony is very short – a minute or two – but a most emotional experience, confronted as the visitor is by thousands of names carved on the panels. Amongst those commemorated here are the Canadians with no known grave and who were killed in Belgium.

The tourist office sells a useful map of the town, with places of interest marked on it; it is a handy document, not least because it will help you master the extraordinary one way system that came into effect a few years ago.

The most useful map for navigation is in the French Green Series, the 1:100000 Lille Dunkirk map, number 2. The War Graves Commission has an office in Ypres at 82 Elverdingestraat (the road that runs past St George's Memorial Church). You may purchase there a Michelin 1:200000 overprinted map with the bulk of the cemeteries marked on it. The sheet number you want for this area is 51, Calais Lille Bruxelles. They also have details of all those buried on the Western Front, and with suitable basic information they should be able to tell you where a person is buried or commemorated.

For details about larger scale maps, see the section relating to touring the battalefield.

The trench maps required are 28 NE 1 (Zonnebeke) and 20 SE 3 (Westroosebeke). They are obtainable from the Imperial War Museum and, for members, from the Trench Map service of the Western Front Association. Trench maps were updated on a regular basis, especially when a major battle was under way, and so there are a range of dates to choose from; but ones dated in the autumn of 1917 are those which will be most useful.

To reach Passchendaele from Ypres the easiest way is probably to find your way out to the Menin Road (signposted Menen) and at the big roundabout (Hell Fire Corner) follow the signs to the A19 motorway. Drive over this and you will come out at another roundabout – turn right into Zonnebeke, drive through the village, and at the top of the ridge (another roundabout) turn left and on to Passchendaele (Passendaele). Returning you can go back the same way, but instead of following the road to Hell Fire Corner (on the line of the old Ypres – Roulers railway line) continue straight on through Frezenberg and Potijze, the Zonnebeke road frequently mentioned in the literature of the war. Alternatively you can return via Bellevue, Gravenstafel and Wieltje, which was the other artery to the Front Line.

I would suggest that you make a car tour of the area covered by this book first, if only to get your bearings. If you are going to walk, sturdy shoes are essential at any time of the year, and walking boots in winter. Wellingtons are too uncomfortable, and so long as you are willing to engage in one or two athletic leaps across a more than usually rutted and muddy track, they are not necessary.

You should have a camera, preferably with a telephoto lens of some sort; and a notebook to record what you have taken a picture of! I would recommend a green card and comprehensive insurance for yourself and the car, and at the least a form E 1 11 to cover the medical side of things. There is still plenty of rusty iron around (leave old munitions alone!) and so ensure that your tetanus jab is up to date. Please keep to tracks and respect the livelihood of the farmers, their crops and their stock.

Passchendaele and area

There is B & B accommodation in Passchendaele, 00 32 (if outside Belgium) 51 771738; prefix this and any other Belgium numbers with a 0 if ringing inside the country. There is also a hotel in the main square in Passchendaele, the Hotel St Joris, which has eight rooms en suite, Phone 00 32 51 778016; Fax 00 32 51 771868 .

Eating at lunchtime is not all that easy as Belgian and French cafés both have an annoying tendency to be closed at the vital hour; so try early or late, or you will not be able, in my experience, to get anything very substantial. Local information may be obtained from the enormously helpful Tourist Information Office in Zonnebeke, which is close to the church in the centre of town and is well signposted with plenty of useful brochures available in English.

There is an excellent museum in Zonnebeke, housed in the imposing building next to the Tourist Office. It has difficult hours of opening:

1 April - 11 November: Weds and Sat 2-6pm
                                     Sundays 10 - 12 and 2 - 6 pm
July and August   Open daily (except Monday) 2 - 6 pm
                                     Sunday openings as above

A word of warning about Mondays in Belgium; they bear a remarkable resemblance to the old British Sunday, and hardly anything appears to be open. More shops now do open, but be warned.

TABLE OF MAPS

The village of Passchendaele taken in June 1917, prior to the devastation caused by the Third Battle of Ypres. See page 94.

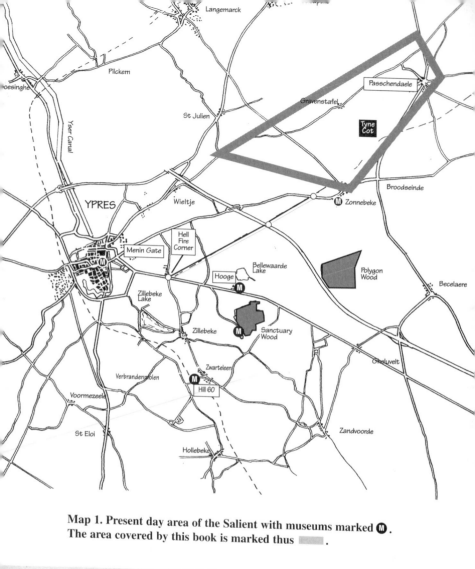

Map 1. Present day area of the Salient with museums marked .
The area covered by this book is marked thus ▬ **.**

Map labels:
Langemarck, Pilckem, oesinghe, Yser Canal, YPRES, St Julien, Wieltje, Hell Fire Corner, Menin Gate, Zillebeke Lake, Zillebeke, Hooge, Bellewaarde Lake, Sanctuary Wood, Verbrandenmolen, Zwarteleen, Hill 60, Voormezeele, St Eloi, Hollebeke, Gravenstafel, Passchendaele, Tyne Cot, Zonnebeke, Broodseinde, Polygon Wood, Becelaere, Gheluvelt, Zandvoorde

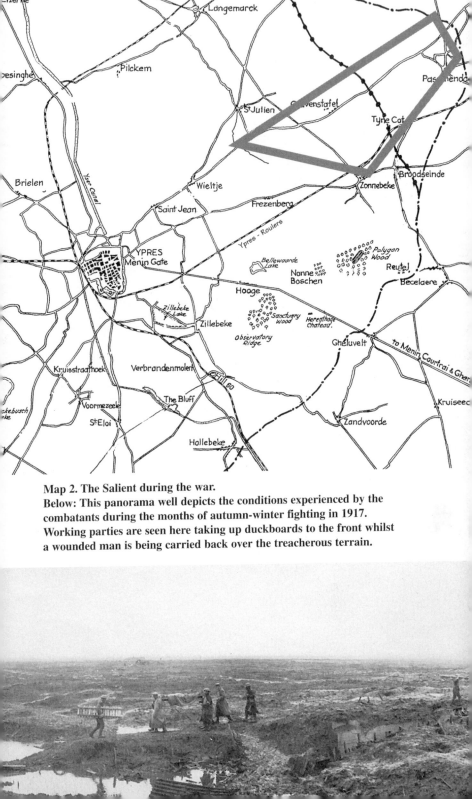

Map 2. The Salient during the war.
Below: This panorama well depicts the conditions experienced by the
combatants during the months of autumn-winter fighting in 1917.
Working parties are seen here taking up duckboards to the front whilst
a wounded man is being carried back over the treacherous terrain.

**Just one of the thousands of German casualties suffered during the
Third Battle of Ypres.**

Chapter One

NEW ZEALAND'S CONTRIBUTION
4 - 12 OCTOBER 1917
1. The battle of Broodseinde 4 October 1917

The New Zealand Division, part of II ANZAC (Australian and New Zealand Army Corps) Corps, had spent a number of months in the area between Armentières and Ypres since their important contribution to the Battle of the Somme. The Division had been involved at Messines in June 1917 and in the Battle of Polygon Wood in the dying days of September. From these triumphs the Corps was moved north to take part in the removal of the Germans from Passchendaele Ridge. For nine months, from May 1917 until February 1918, the New Zealand Division was 'super heavy', ie it had sixteen battalions in four brigades instead of the customary twelve in three brigades. This goes some way to explaining its heavy usage during the battle. For the attack II ANZAC took over the front of V Corps, part of Fifth Army; the area was some seventeen miles long, with a Corps frontage of two miles narrowing to under a mile in the rear, with all the problems this provided with confined road communications.

At this stage in the battle of Third Ypres the British Front now constituted a marked salient. The right was placed on the high ground about the Menin Road, moving from there to Polygon Wood but then curved inwards from Zonnebeke to the east of St Julien and Langemark before curving back sharply before Houthoulst Forest. The next phase of the battle would be carried out in bounds, with the aim of capturing the Passchendaele Ridge; because of the lateness of the season there was a need for urgency.

This first bound became known as the Battle of Broodseinde, 4 October 1917. It was an attack along a seven mile front. The New Zealanders would be attacking with their fellow members of II ANZAC, 3rd Australian Division; their boundary with I ANZAC was the Ypres – Roulers railway.

The Germans had altered their strategy to deal with attacks – reverses suffered on the Somme and at Messines as well as the heavy casualties suffered as a consequence of the concentration of artillery meant that a policy of holding forward trenches lightly and of abandoning continuous lines of trenches in places, was adopted. These were substituted with a mixture of pill-boxes which mutually supported each other as well as isolated machine-gun groups posted in

The Ninth Company of 3/Wellington Regiment in Belgium.

Map 3. The ground over which the New Zealanders attacked during the Battle of Broodseinde. The Germans had altered their methods in dealing with attacks – instead of holding continuous trench lines they built concrete pill boxes which provided mutual support.

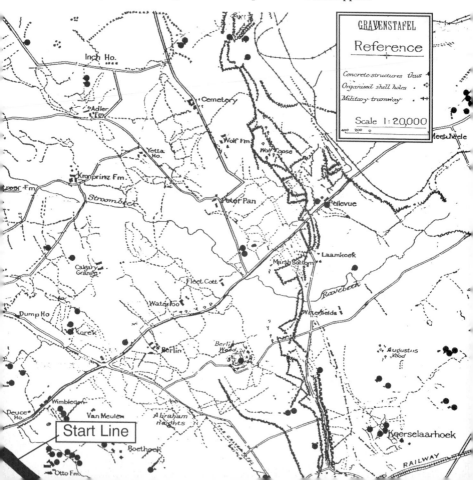

shell holes, protected by bands of wire. The pill-boxes were of varying sizes, the larger in the earlier days being called in the British popular press 'field forts'. Most were not much bigger than nine feet square, made of reinforced concrete with overhead cover of between three and six feet and were essentially indestructible unless by a direct hit from a heavy calibre gun. They were small targets and even if spotted by aerial photography (from the tracks leading to them) they were usually so camouflaged that it was difficult for artillery observers either to see them or report if a shell had hit them. These pill-boxes were scattered in an irregular manner according to the advantages of the ground; but

A German soldier attempts to contact his comrades in a bunker that has had its entrance buried during heavy shelling.

New Zealand memorial   North end of Abraham Heights

Photographed from the site of Dochy Farm. The New Zealanders attacked across this ground.

there were also regular lines of such defences where 'traditionally' there might have been expected to be a defensive trench line system.

The main physical objectives of the New Zealand attack were the Gravenstafel and Bellevue spurs, two of a number of such features that ran out westwards/north westwards from the main Passchendaele ridge that stood dominant over the ground that fell away towards Ypres.

A New Zealand artillery battery supports the attack. Note the mules with panniers for carrying eight 18 pounder shells.

The capture of this ridge would provide relatively dominating positions (and at least secure much of the Salient from direct German observation) as well as giving the possibility of reasonably drained and habitable trenches for the remainder of the winter. It would also be a more practicable position from which to launch an offensive the following Spring.

A successful attack on the ridge in one bound was considered to be impractical, the problem being that of effective artillery support, and so the first onslaught was to be (for the New Zealanders) the spur which included 's Graventafel and Abraham Heights, a name given to this prominence by the Canadians at the time of the Second Battle of Ypres in April 1915.

According to the German account, *Flandern 1917*, 4 October was the first of the black days of the German Army. The artillery preparation was considered to be excellent and at the end of the day the New Zealand Division had captured their objectives, almost 1200 prisoners and fifty-nine machine guns. They now looked across the valley towards the German positions on Bellevue Spur known as the Flanders I Line. See map page 122

The boundary between 1 and 4 Brigade was practically the Wieltje to Passchendaele road. Even today the landscape is quite featureless;

A telephone wire from HQ leads to a NZ gun position, situated in a featureless mud bath.

TAYLOR LIBRARY

Map 4

A section of a German Trench map depicting how they mapped the area and marked their defences.

under the constant shelling of the last weeks, not to mention the battles of 1914 and 1915, the buildings and copses that might have aided orientation were mere shadows of themselves. Close by where the ruins of such places as Dochy Farm, Riverside, Otto Farm. Boethoek and Waterloo had stood lay scattered pill-boxes. The small streams that dealt with the waters coming down the spurs had been – or were in the process of being – transformed into marshy quagmires and became significant obstacles in subsequent phases of the battle.

The two leading battalions of 4 Brigade were 3/Auckland on the right and 3/Otago on the left followed by 3/Canterbury and 3/Wellington. Whilst the various British units were moving into position the Germans were also planning a counter-strike of their own, aiming to remove the British from the Ypres-Roulers railway and reaching out to Zonnebeke and Polygon Wood. They did not consider that the British artillery would be ready yet for a further onslaught and hoped to capture their enemy off balance. Their artillery barrage commenced at 5.20 am, forty minutes before that of their attackers, and this caused some considerable casualties to the attacking ANZAC divisions (the Australians were to the right of the New Zealanders) – the response was to push their men forward to the limits of the planned British shrapnel barrage. At 6 am the British barrage fell; how things had changed from that of 1 July 1916.

'There were four distinct artillery barrages in addition to a machine-gun barrage, to take the assaulting columns forward, break up counter-attacks and protect the infantry on the captured objectives. They covered a depth of a thousand yards. Nearest the advancing lines was a creeping shrapnel barrage of the field guns; beyond it a stationary curtain of fire was provided by the light howitzers and a proportion of the field guns. At increasing distances from the advancing infantry a third barrage was given by the 6 inch howitzers and a fourth by 60-pounders, 8 inch and 9.2 inch howitzers.'[1]

The work of the artillery often does not receive the attention that has been bestowed upon the infantry, strange considering the vital part that it played in the war. A New Zealand gunner wrote home:

'Those who heard it say it was tremendous, the din, but we in the pit heard it not at all, or only in a subconscious way, to be remembered afterwards, heard nothing but the vicious whanging of our own guns, nothing but the jerk of the breach as it opened and the snap as it closed again, nothing but the clang of falling "empties" and the rattle of the live shells as the No 4 [a member of the gun team] jammed them on, nothing but the ticking of the watch covering the interval between the rounds and the No 1's voice: "Thirty more left! Elevate five minutes! Drop one hundred!" then the watch's ticking again till he opened his mouth once more, and before the "Fire!" had hardly left it, the spiteful tonguing of the gun, her rattle and quiver as she settled down, and the hiss of the buffer coming home. ...As the range lengthened and her nose pointed further skyward the brute [ie

A New Zealand 4.5 howitzer team in action.

his gun] *got worse, and between sticking trail and sticking buffer, the sweat came down in streams, blinding my eyes and tasting salt to my tongue; but we got there with the best, neither skipped nor lagged behind. Of the two, that last is the greater crime. For a late shot in the lifting barrage often means death to many of our fellows.'*

The Germans had not been entirely idle in their artillery response, and in fact a barrage that they put on the Zonnebeke-Langemarck road, which was accompanied by a heavy machine-gun barrage on the same area, caused considerable casualties to 2/Wellington on the left of 1 Brigade; otherwise the German artillery was relatively ineffectual.

It was recognised that the Hannebeek, a small stream that ran along the front of 4 Brigade, was likely to cause problems, and the barrage was halted here to allow the men to cross the quagmire which had the dangerous added element of shellholes filled with water. In fact the stream and the marsh around it was picked through without too much difficulty and the following battalions suffered from the German defensive barrage which naturally enough also had this natural obstacle as a defensive barrage line.

The men of the brigade pressed on, eager to keep under the shelter of the barrage, leaving parties to deal with isolated German garrisons in their pill boxes; thus men of 3/Otago captured a machine gun and fifty prisoners from the defences at Van Meulen. Their target was the Red Line, and they knew they had reached it when the barrage in front had smoke (fired by one gun from each battery).

The barrage now fired for about an hour on a line 150 yards ahead of this point (the Red Line) and the time was used to consolidate and remove the remaining German defenders; pill-boxes were particularly plentiful on the right of the attack, to the south and beyond Abraham Heights. Those Germans who did not at once surrender, in the laconic words of the New Zealand history, 'were shot'. 3/Otago captured the ruins of Gravenstafel and had a haul of some hundred prisoners.

The advance on 4 Brigade front was continued by 3/Canterbury on the right and 3/Wellington on the left. The barrage was now to advance (from 8.10 am) fifty yards every four minutes; whilst the commanding heights of Bellevue Spur were to be blinded by the use of smoke, which helped them but did not prevent the Germans pouring down

A German machine-gun position captured by the New Zealanders.

considerable machine-gun fire upon them as they crested the lower slope.

3/Canterbury had left their billets at Goldfish Château [on the right of the railway line crossing on the road from Ypres to Vlamertinge, just outside the western outskirts of Ypres] at 5 pm on 3 October. They had moved up to Pommern Castle at 11 pm that night; they followed on behind 3/Auckland. There were some problems with German pill-boxes in Berlin Wood (sometimes known as Berlin Copse), but these were captured and the battalion soon dug in on its new position (the Blue Dotted Line), although it suffered harassing fire and sniping from Bellevue spur to the north east. Battalion headquarters were established at Boethoek, on the west side of Abraham Heights. The battalion remained holding the line until the evening of 5 October, having constructed traversed trenches to a depth of four feet six. The attack had cost it over 250 casualties, but with the comparatively small number of fifty dead.

To its left 3/Wellington had continued the advance beyond Gravenstafel and down into the valley formed by the Ravebeek and Stroombeek. They suffered considerable casualties, particularly amongst the officers and senior NCOs – indeed there was only one sergeant who was neither killed nor wounded. Much of the heaviest fighting took place around Waterloo, a position just to the north of the Passchendaele road.

1 Brigade had a similarly successful time, although 2/Wellington suffered many casualties amongst their senior officers on the slopes below Korek. The two front battalions, 1/Auckland and 1/Wellington had become separated, with the left hand battalion, 1/Auckland, veering too far left to deal with Boetleer, which left a gap between them and 1/Wellington trying to deal with the Germans at Korek. Two dugouts [ie in this case pill-boxes whose roofs were almost at ground level] on the crest of the village caused considerable difficulties, and thus parties from 1/Wellington and 3/Otago rushed forward under the British barrage and threw grenades into the pill-box entrances to neutralise the occupants. The Wellington Regiment history tells the story,

> 'One of these pill-boxes was fairly large and must have been of some importance. Sergeant A Paterson entered to find some thirty Germans dead or dying from the havoc our bombs had wrought. There seemed to be an inner recess in which was a German major with some men. As soon as Sergeant Paterson entered the German officer set fire to a mass of papers with some

incendiary material. In a moment the whole place was in flame [and] Sergeant Paterson came out; but the Germans were all incinerated. This dugout burned for hours afterwards.[2]

The line was eventually secured with many individual feats of heroism as junior officers and NCOs dealt with pockets of the enemy and action was taken to dig into the position. Behind the supporting battalions followed, ready to jump on to the next objective. 2/Wellington suffered as it prepared to come forward to the Red Line, losing a company commander, Captain HT Boscawen (buried at Tyne Cot), almost immediately. Worse was to follow soon afterwards as the commanding officer, Lieutenant-Colonel CH Weston, was severely wounded by a piece of shell.

It was in this sector of the divisional front that the planned attack of the Germans was most evident; a double line of shell holes about three hundred yards apart was found to have two to four dead Germans in each one. These men had been massed for their attack and were hit by

German soldiers caught by shell fire in the initial barrage.

the opening British barrage. The worst resistance that this battalion faced (on the left of the divisional attack) was around Kronprinz Farm. A short piece of trench in front of it was captured at the point of the bayonet whilst the farm itself had been used as a battalion headquarters; the ferocity of the attack left the attackers with important plans and papers which there had not been sufficient time to destroy. The battalion set about consolidating its line and set up its headquarters in the ruins of Boetleer.

The Battle of Broodseinde had been a great success; 5,000 prisoners had been captured (New Zealand Division 1150) and Passchendaele Ridge had been secured at its southern end. German tactics had been put into disarray, as their High Command wrestled with the problem of how best to fight a successful defensive battle in the face of limited objectives supported by heavy artillery. Attempts to fight an elastic defence, with lightly held forward trenches and the use of reserves to launch a counter-attack when the enemy were off balance were deemed to have failed at the Battle of the Menin Road the previous month; reverting to a heavily held front line system seemed to have brought no better results.

The New Zealand Division commemorates this battle with one of its cenotaph memorials at the Gravenstafel cross-roads. The Division was not to remember the attacks of the next few days so warmly.

1 *The New Zealand Division* 1916–1919
2 *The Wellington Regiment NZEF*

A New Zealander examines a captured pill-box. Many were used by the British as battalion HQs and aid posts. Entrances were facing the wrong way and in some cases they underwent modification – they were 'turned'.
TAYLOR LIBRARY

Chapter Two

NEW ZEALAND'S FAILURE:
THE ATTACK OF 12 OCTOBER 1917
Prelude: The Battle of Poelcapelle, 9 October 1917

The New Zealand division was not involved in this battle. Its front was taken over by the 49th (1/West Riding) Division with the 66th (2/East Lancs) on its right The decision to continue the battle at this stage is one of the most controversial of the war, but it is no part of this book to get involved in this controversy. Put briefly, Haig felt that every advantage should be taken of a situation in which the enemy seemed to be in considerable disarray. Until 4 October no insurmountable problems had been reported in supplying the troops at the front and maintaining the weight of artillery (as was amply proved by the attack on that day). It was deemed that prospects were reasonable enough to bring elements of the cavalry within striking reach of the front. But everything depended upon the weather.

The rain started on the afternoon of the 4th and continued through to the 7th, on which day there were heavy squalls. The Army Commanders (Fifth, Gough and Second, Plumer) told Haig that evening that they could continue but would prefer to close the campaign down for the winter. He decided against this for a variety of reasons, one of which was the better ground and communications that would be obtained by occupying the Westroosebeke-Passchendaele ridge. The plan of attack on 9 October was made less ambitious and indeed the weather improved significantly for much of the 8th; however the rain returned that afternoon.

The communications situation had become almost impossible; plank roads disappeared into the mud and the valley in which II ANZAC found themselves was a 'porridge of mud'. Men were out in the open, guns were got as far forward as possible (which was not far enough) and were concentrated in small areas almost adjacent to what passed for a road, making them vulnerable to counter-battery fire and aerial bombing. There was little or no shelter and the whole place had become a featureless landscape where mud was the dominant characteristic. Trying to move at all in such conditions was depressingly difficult and perhaps this phase of the battle more than any other was to give Passchendaele its reputation of a heroic but futile battle against both the elements and the Germans.

The most serious problem was that faced by the artillery. Guns could not be brought forward without extraordinary difficulty and in fact the effort often had to be abandoned. Guns which had seen plenty of service were in need of overhaul, which was quite impossible in the circumstances. It was not just a matter of bringing up the guns but also the enormous quantities of ammunition that were required – and this had to be cleaned before it could be fired. Water was, naturally, in very short supply. Animals suffered tremendously, often disappearing into the mud (or at least having to be abandoned and shot) when they slipped off the plank roads; whilst they were covered in muck, with no adequate standings and with fodder and water in short supply.

The guns themselves required stable platforms if they were to provide any form of adequate protection for the infantry and counter-battery fire against the German guns. In fact the field guns would only just be able to cover the objective for 9 October, assuming that they had stable platforms, and were unable to reach Passchendaele village at all, around and about which many of the German field batteries were positioned. The heavy artillery suffered from similar problems of moving up to a satisfactory gun-line, and many of the personnel were extremely tired, a shortage meaning that exhaustion was becoming a

The view from Bellevue Spur looking south and southwest. This gives some idea of how important a vantage point this was to the Germans.

Lamkeek Farm   Augustus Farm   Tyne Cot

severe problem. In addition the German bombers were active at night time, and whilst not particularly effective in terms of damage (and the Royal Flying Corps was giving as good as it got) they added to the pressures and tensions of the battlefield. The Official History summarises the situation thus:

> 'The chief cause of the great discontent during this period of the Flanders fighting was, in fact, the continuous demands on regimental officers and men to carry out tasks which appeared physically impossible to perform, and which no other army could have faced. It must be emphasised again, too, that in all that vast wilderness of slime hardly tree, hedge, wall or building could be seen. As at the Somme no landmarks existed, nor any scrap of natural cover other than the mud-filled shell holes. That the attacks ordered were so gallantly made in such conditions stands to the immortal credit of the battalions concerned.'

To put it mildly, the attack was far from a success; elsewhere, to the north and the south, there had been some gain of ground, but in general this was the Germans' day. The decision was made that another attempt would have to be made on Passchendaele. This was to take place on 12 October.

The New Zealand advance on 4 October put them on the eastern edge of Berlin Wood, facing the quagmire of Marsh Bottom.

Hamburg   Berlin Wood   Marsh Bottom

The First Battle of Passchendaele, 12 October 1917

The objectives for II ANZAC were to be the same as on 9 October, except that the attack was to be by Russell's New Zealand Division on the left (thus occupying almost exactly the position they had left on 5 October) whilst Monash's 3rd Australian did the same on the right. The New Zealand Division had as its objective the Bellevue spur and the area north and east of Goudberg whilst the Australians occupied the eastern end of Passchendaele itself.

For this battle the Official History allows just over six pages; the action of the New Zealand Division merits some thirty lines (not that British or Australian divisions merit any more space); this compares with the considerable attention devoted to this disaster in New Zealand formation and unit histories. These concentrate on individual acts of heroism and on the distressing subject of the problems of getting the wounded cleared away to safety.

The bare outline of the battle can, indeed, be told simply. General Plumer, before he was fully aware of the facts, reported to GHQ (General Head Quarters) on the evening of 9 October that he expected to replace the ANZAC Corps after they had captured the ridge on 12 October with the Canadians, fresh to the battlefield, on 14 October. These men would be able to continue the advance ever eastwards and

threaten the vital German railheads at Roulers and Thourout. The reason for this unlikely optimism, that the ridge would be captured so straightforwardly, lay in a misapprehension about the reasons for the failure of the 9 October attack, which was put down to the mud. In fact the German positions were formidable in new wire entanglements many yards deep, pill-boxes and manpower – matters that were reported by the patrols of men such as Sergeant Travis, a New Zealander who enjoyed the nickname the 'King of No Man's Land' due to his skill and audacity in exploring this most feared part of the battlefield.

'King of No
Man's Land'
Sergeant Travis

'The situation was as poor for the artillery as it had been on 9 October – conceivably worse. The rain continued to come down in the form of showers, and it was cold. It was extremely difficult to make progress with the plank roads, especially as so much of the labour for this, despite a willing spirit, was suffering from fatigue. The field batteries were unable to advance further, and the heavy batteries, in vain efforts to move to forward positions, found little time for counter-battery work or for destroying the wire and pill-boxes on Wallemolen spur. Both wire entanglement and pillboxes could be seen from Gravenstafel

spur, and the forward liaison officers with infantry brigades pressed throughout the day for their destruction by heavy artillery before the assault was launched. No action, however, could be taken until the late afternoon, when a few heavy batteries opened up on the Bellevue sector for a short time, but with negligible results.[2]

The battle opened at 5.25 am in wind and drizzle; this soon turned into heavy rain for most of the rest of the day. The barrage was very poor – almost insignificant, and the floundering soldiers soon lost whatever cover it might have provided. Pinned down by the uncut thick bands of wire and by heavy and accurate machine-gun fire, the two attacking brigades, each on a battalion front, got almost nowhere, except for a gain of a few hundred yards on the left. Attempts to renew the attack in the afternoon were cancelled, largely on the initiative of the remaining battalion commanders. The rest of the day, and the subsequent forty-eight hours or so, were spent in retrieving the wounded under the most appalling conditions.

'This splendid division lost a hundred officers and 2,635 other ranks within a few hours in brave but vain attempts – its only failure – to carry out a task beyond the power of any infantry with so little support, and had gained no ground except on the left.'[3]

2 Brigade was to provide the left divisional front, its axis of advance being, to all intents and purposes, the Mosselmarkt road, which itself ran along the central, western part of the Bellevue spur. The attack was to be in a series of bounds, with the 750 yard frontage being filled by a battalion (2/Otago), followed by 1/Otago then 1/Canterbury with the Brigade reserve, 2/Canterbury following in the wake of the leading two battalions to provide extra manpower when needed and to cover the flanks if the attacking brigades on either side failed to keep up.

On the night of 10 October 2/Otago moved up to the line; the scene that greeted them was indescribable,

'The whole countryside, under the continuous rain and heavy shelling, was rapidly approaching the state of a deep morass through which the relieving troops blindly floundered in the darkness of night until they reached the position which was only nominally a front line. There was overwhelming and gruesome evidence of the disastrous results of the British attack launched on the 9th. To say nothing of the dead, scores of men, wounded and near to death, still lay out over the country, unattended and without protection from the weather. 148 Brigade, so heavy were

An artist's impression of the attack on Passchendaele village. This appeared in *The Illustrated War News* of 21 November 1917.

its losses, had apparently found it impossible to cope with the task of clearing the wounded. At Waterloo Farm the congestion was such that many of the wounded were still lying above ground and in the open, and frequently enemy shells burst among or near them and put an end to their miseries. There were probably 200 stretcher cases lying over the area, and it was doubtful if any

'Floundering to victory through the mud of Flanders: The normal state of the battlefields.'

of them had been fed until our troops provided them with rations on the morning of the 11th.'

Reconnaissance by, amongst others, the indomitable Sergeant Travis, in front of the Otago line, revealed the strength of the German position, which included six large pill-boxes on the battalion front. It suggested that bodies of Germans, about a dozen in number, used the wire surrounded block houses as shelter at night time and occupied shell holes before them to form the German front line. The commanding officer asked, early on the morning of the 11th, that heavy artillery be brought to bear on these strong points. 'After a lengthy period of time the heavy artillery opened out on the Bellevue Spur, but only briefly, and the damage done was negligible.' This response was a grim warning of the ineffectual artillery cover that was available to the attack; not so much a fault of the artillery but a consequence of the ground conditions and difficulties of transport to the rear of the New Zealand front.

The battalions moved forward in the early hours of the 12th, laid out in a perilously shallow area caused by the need to get the men across the Ravebeek, which had become an impassable morass which had effectively only one narrow duck board crossing over it. Across a width of about seven hundred or so yards and to a depth of a hundred yards were crammed some two thousand men.

The artillery were to provide a barrage to protect the assault. The regimental history notes:

> '...normally, exclusive of heavy guns and heavy and medium howitzers, the operation would have been supported by 144 18-pounders and 48 4.5-inch howitzers. The difficulties of complying with the demands of the prepared plan of artillery co-operation were so great that there could not be ensured even the efficient support of anything approaching that number of guns – probably less than half.'

The attack was launched at 5.25 am; the artillery fire was very weak, and even worse was falling behind the start line, causing considerable casualties to 1/Otago, one of the follow-up battalions. After the misery of a night of lying in the bogland and under persistent rain in chilling conditions, the men rose to face a torrent of machine-gun fire from the security of their pill-boxes. At the moment the attack commenced a heavy German barrage fell fifty metres or so to the west of the Ravebeek and in the vicinity of Waterloo Farm. This housed the battalion headquarters of all four battalions in 2 Brigade as well as being the site of a major Aid Post.

The combination of fire from the Germans threatened to end the attack almost before it began; on the left the artillery barrage, as a consequence of one of its lifts, which were of about fifty yards, had completely missed the pill-boxes in the vicinity of Peter Pan. Two pill-boxes on the crest proved particularly lethal, despite the best attempts to come to grips with them through the wire. The German gunners in

Runners setting out from Company HQ, housed in a captured German pill box, during the offensive by the New Zealanders. TAYLOR LIBRARY

here effectively managed to stop a company of reinforcements coming up to the line a thousand yards away to the left. To add to the German artillery and machine-gun fire were the extremely effective activities of the selective fire of snipers scattered amongst the shell holes.

1/Otago now came into the picture and tried to crawl through the wire in order to get to close with the machine gunners in their concrete fortresses; away to the far left the twenty eight unwounded members of 10th Company managed to dig themselves in to the remnants of Wolf Copse, in fact beyond the brigade boundary. This was practically the total of tangible success on this flank.

On the right, 8th Company 1/Otago came on behind the men of 2/Otago to find few of these men left. This was partly as a result of casualties and partly because the advance had veered too far to the north. This had left the right flank exposed to the completely uncovered fire from two pill-boxes, about a hundred yards apart, close to the Ravebeek. The Company Commander, Captain RH Nicholson, was killed almost the moment the advance began [he is buried at Passchendaele New Military Cemetery], and his place was taken over by Second Lieutenant AR Cockerell. He determined to take action against these pill-boxes, as otherwise there was no chance of further

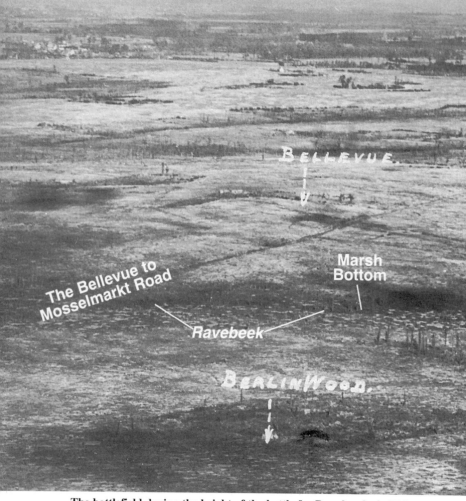

BELLEVUE

Marsh Bottom

The Bellevue to Mosselmarkt Road

Ravebeek

BERLIN WOOD

The battlefield during the height of the battle for Passchendaele Ridge, taken looking north, northeast. Compare with photographs pages 32-33.

progress being made on this sector of the battalion's attack. By this stage there was confusion and dislocation in the company, with every man seeking cover where he could. Cockerell found himself isolated. The regimental history records his subsequent actions in a tone filled with admiration at his audacity and courage.

'*Continuing his advance, he was ultimately confronted by a short length of trench which extended across the foremost block-house. Along this trench line approximately forty of the enemy were established, but so rapid and continuous had been their fire against the flank of our attack that their ammunition was completely expended, and when confronted and called upon to*

40

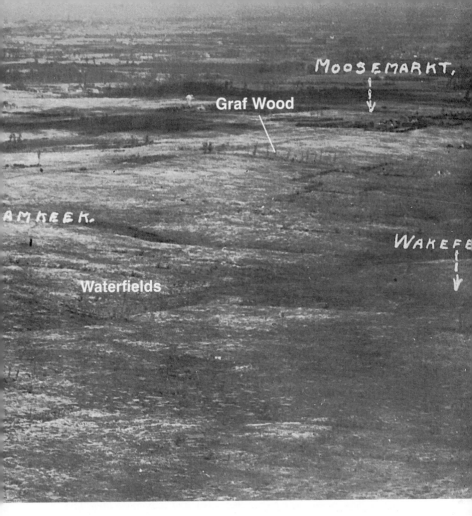

MOOSEMARKT.

Graf Wood

AMKEEK.

WAKEFE

Waterfields

surrender they filed out of their post with hands above their heads and slowly trekked back as prisoners through our lines. A distance of but twenty yards ahead was the first block-house, into which those of the enemy who were without had rushed for shelter. Reaching this pill-box still unscathed, this single officer bayoneted six of the garrison as they emerged from it at the rear, and then forced the surrender of the remainder and sent them back as prisoners. He was now joined by Private G Harris, from his company, who, carrying with him a Lewis gun, had struggled forward out of the confusion of 8th Company's shattered attack. With valorous determination both advanced to the attack of the

A busy scene on the Menin Road during the Third Battle of Ypres. Prisoners are being brought in and a 'Jock' can be seen escorting Germans supporting a wounded soldier to an aid post.

second and larger block-house, approximately a hundred yards distance. This concrete stronghold was found to contain a garrison of two officers and thirty men with two machine guns. Their guns had ceased to fire, the apparent reason, remarkable as it may seem, being that they also had expended their last round of ammunition, a further indication of the unceasing destruction directed against our troops from the time the attack opened until it had been effectively smashed. The whole of this garrison were also made prisoners and the two machine guns destroyed. This represented a total capture of over eighty prisoners, two block-houses with their machine guns, and a length of enemy trench.'

Soon after this he was joined by members of 3rd Australian Division, on the New Zealanders' immediate right. An officer and six men joined up with Cockerell and they now decided that the best thing to do was to try and arrange a flanking attack on the Bellevue Spur, catching the defences in the rear. However four runners were killed in an attempt to take a report back to Battalion Headquarters and it was decided that all that could be done was to consolidate the gains. Cockerell returned to reorganise the remnants of the battalion, who were left in what was No Man's Land only a few yards in front of their original position. In due course he was awarded the DSO, a rare honour for one of so junior a rank.

Meanwhile members of 1/Canterbury Regiment had continued to advance in support. Their commanding officer, Lieutenant-Colonel GA King, DSO* was killed very soon after crossing the stream [he is buried in Ypres Reservoir Cemetery] and they got no further forward than their predecessors. Gaps in the wire were deliberate German fire traps, and of course the covering barrage had disappeared off to the east, where it did these men no good whatsoever. It was quite clear to those on the ground here

A R Cockerell, DSO

that the wire and the bunkers had first to be destroyed before further effective action could be taken; whilst the battalions that had taken part in the attack at this point were in a fearful state of intermingled confusion and dislocation.

To 2 Brigade's left were the four battalions of the New Zealand Rifle Brigade and to their left 9th (Scottish) Division. The lead battalion was 2/NZRB which had taken over the line on the night of 10/11 October. The situation was so confused here that they took over a line which was held by men from six different units of 49th Division. As for 2 Brigade, the attack was to be launched in depth, fronted by one battalion. Brigade Headquarters was situated in an old German pill-box to the north of Gravenstafel at Korek. As the attack was launched it was quite clear that the barrage, 'so pitifully weak as to be barely perceptible', according to the regimental history, was to be of no avail.

The main German defensive fire came from their extremely well placed machine guns – the German barrage was not particularly heavy and consisted for the most part of high explosive shells, whose destructive capacity was considerably reduced by the mud. The battalion soon became bogged down, whilst the valley on the right of the attack became a death trap. Even now, eighty years later, it is open and devoid of cover, vulnerable to fire from Bellevue Spur and from the high ground to the north. The men tended to bunch to the right, to get behind Wolf Farm and use this high ground as a means of getting around the German defenders. This meant that a gap of 400 yards opened up between the two attacking brigades. An attempt was made by elements of 2 Brigade to remove a German bunker on the Bellevue Spur that was largely responsible for causing this gap between them, but they were unable to get through the wire that defended it. It was the remnants of these men, mentioned earlier, who established a post on the western side of Wolf Copse. This at least ensured that there was a reasonably secure connection between the flanks of the two brigades.

Because of the intense fire that was hitting 2/NZRB from the two flanks the attack's forward momentum all but ceased – in any case such a move was seemingly utterly impossible because of a line of concrete pill-boxes defended by wide bands of wire. The direction of attack swung away to the left, towards the Wallemolen cemetery. Although relatively fresh troops arrived from the following battalions, it was quite clear that no further forward progress was a practical possibility.

The cemetery itself was captured with some difficulty; twenty five of the garrison in the strong point in it were killed and three captured along with four machine guns. The position was important and helped to ensure that at least some tangible progress was made in this sector. Soon after 8 am the attack had effectively come to a halt; the three attacking battalions had lost the majority of their officers, the men were mixed up and even some members of the 9th (Scottish) Division were in amongst them. The history records that

> 'all ranks were drenched to the skin and plastered with shell-hole slime from head to foot; a large proportion of the rifles and Lewis guns were choked with mud; and, taking advantage of the decrease in the volume of our fire, the enemy was rapidly reinforcing his forward line and even placing machine-guns on the top of pill-boxes.'

The commanding officer of 2/NZRB examined the positions gained and decided that the line should be consolidated where the advance had halted; this was about five hundred yards forward from the start line on the left and two hundred yards on the right.

However, the attack on the left and the right of the New Zealanders had been relatively – at least at first – rather more successful, and instructions were issued by Division that the attack should be resumed at 3 pm, with more limited objectives. The battalion commanders were called back for a conference at Kronprinz Farm (which also served as the main Aid Post) at 1 pm. Here they all protested at the proposal, but were over-ruled. The time spent in going to and fro meant that they only had half an hour or so to organise their scattered men for a new onslaught. Fortunately the attack was halted once it was realised that the gains had not been as widespread as first reported.

2 Brigade had been faced with a similar quandary when the instructions for a new attack came up. The battalion commanders similarly protested. The men were exhausted; the casualties, particularly amongst officers and NCOs were very heavy; the ground was in a horrific state; whilst many of the men were so tied up in the wire that they could only be got out before a new and essential barrage in darkness if further huge losses were to be avoided.

The tragic problem that now faced the two brigades was that of the evacuation of the wounded. The subject is dealt with in depth by all the New Zealand histories, but that of the Otago Regiment deserves to be quoted in full.

'Hundreds of badly wounded men lay out over the front of No Man's Land, exposed to the added miseries of mud and weather. The stretcher service, extended though it had been, was unequal to the task of dealing with such abnormal losses under conditions of movement presenting tremendous difficulties. Over 200 cases which had been carried down to Waterloo Farm had remained there throughout the day awaiting evacuation under intermittent shell fire, and several were killed. Others who had vainly endeavoured to struggle down from the line sank into shell-holes and, weighted down by the appalling mud and the

Bringing in the wounded, four men to a stretcher, during the battle.

The grim results of war – British dead gathered for identification prior to burial.

burden of their wounds, many of them never arose again. Such was the state of the ground and the distance to be covered that six men, working in relays, were required to each stretcher.'

Men were commandeered from wherever available to assist with this horrendous task. 1200 men of 4 Brigade were sent forward to assist; men from Division, Army and the Army Service Corps, were pressed into service. A battalion from 147 Brigade was rushed up to help.

'..as darkness came down over the battlefield the stillness of the night was pierced by the agonised cries of the wounded, many of whom must have died before help could reach them. For them the Hell of Passchendaele was ended.'

Site of Wallemolen Cemetery, with Wolf Farm in the background. In the distance, on the horizon, may be seen the rising ground of Bellevue Spur.

The men were carried throughout the following day to Waterloo Farm and from there to Bank Farm.

'These parties worked without interruption from the enemy until 5 o'clock in the evening, moving over No Man's Land as far forward as the German wire. The enemy was also engaged removing his dead and wounded under cover of the Red Cross flag, and thus a sort of armistice prevailed. It was during this period that a German medical officer admitted in course of conversation that they too had suffered heavily, a fact which was evidenced by the exertions of their stretcher bearers. Close on 500 cases required to be carried from the Regimental Aid Post at Waterloo Farm to the Advanced Dressing Post at Spree Farm .... a distance of about two-and-a-half miles, and so torn with shell-holes and deep in mud was the whole of the area that six, and sometimes eight, men working in relays had to be attached to each stretcher.'

The result of all this work was that Waterloo Farm was overflowing with casualties, hopelessly congested, with the men barely better off in terms of medical treatment than when they were stuck out on the battlefield. In extremis the Brigade commander appealed directly to the Divisional commander at 5.45 am on the 14th, ie over forty-eight hours after the attack was launched,

'In spite of frequent appeals to every branch of the Staff, and the ADMS [Assistant Director of Medical Services] *three times, the 75 stretcher cases at Waterloo which I asked the ADMS to arrange the removal of at 12 noon yesterday, are still lying there; 40 of them have been lying out in the open under shell fire the whole night. I am powerless to do more than I have done. As a last extremity I appeal to you personally.'*

Waterloo Farm today, once the site of a Regimental Aid Post, and, during the battle, clogged with wounded who could be given scant attention.

By noon the division had cleared Waterloo Farm; the whole unhappy performance was repeated almost in duplicate at Kronprinz Farm, the Regimental Aid Post on the left of the attack. The New Zealand Division had suffered some 2,730 casualties in the Passchendaele attacks. The missing have their place in the central apse of the Tyne Cot Memorial.

The following days the New Zealanders remained in the line, until replaced by the Canadians. There was one moment of sweet revenge, though, for the battered men of the division. The Wellington Regiment history noted,

> 'One afternoon, one of our long range guns made an attempt to demolish the pill-boxes on the crest of Bellevue Spur, and a remarkably accurate shoot it was too. After the first shot, the pill-box was quickly vacated, and Germans could be seen scurrying across the sky-line. Then, when one of our shots hit the concrete blockhouse fair and square, the ranks of Tuscany could scarce forbear to cheer. A little later, a figure could be seen slowly wending its way down the spur towards us, and a poor shell-shocked German walked right into Auckland's lines.'

1 Official History 1917, Volume 2
2 Ibid.
3 Ibid.

After the attack, New Zealand troops brought out of the Salient by train for a well-deserved rest.

Chapter Three

THE CANADIANS ARRIVE
Their first attack 18 - 26 October 1917

The failure of the attack on 12 October led to a rethink by Haig. He had already decided to move the Canadian Corps to Flanders earlier in the month, to enable him to have a cohesive corps of comparatively fresh troops with an excellent battle record to complete the offensive. He had to work hard to persuade Currie, the Corps commander, who made it clear that he was not prepared to serve under Gough's Fifth Army. The only reasons for considering the offensive were to establish a realistic line of defence for the winter and a good springboard for operations in the spring; to keep the Germans occupied in Flanders whilst preparations further south for the Cambrai Offensive (which took place in November) continued; and to provide indirect support for the first big French offensive (at Malmaison) since their mutinies which had been such a cause of concern throughout the summer.

Haig agreed with Currie that an attack should not take place until he, Currie, was satisfied that the arrangements, particularly of artillery, would ensure a degree of success without excessive casualties. In addition Haig no longer expected the capture of the ridge to be achieved in a single bound but rather in a series of three 'snatch and grab' actions with several days between each one. After some discussion with Haig, Plumer (commanding Second Army) and Currie it was determined that these would take place on 26 and 30 October and 6 November.

A W Currie
Commander of Canadian Corps

A vitally important task was the repair of roads and the creation of new plank tracks that would enable supplies, shells and guns to be brought further forward. Thousands of men were put to this task, aided by a spell of ten days or so of good weather. The Germans hindered operations by frequent barrages of gas shells of different types, generally aimed at disabling rather than killing the soldiers and adding a considerable element of trepidation in their work. It was, of course, also particularly unpleasant for the hundreds of animals that were also on the battle area, hauling up guns, rations, shells and trench supplies as well as the material required for the new plank roads and the heavy tramways.

The artillery position at this stage was not good – as was shown in the previous chapter about the New Zealand attack. The way to the left and right sections of the corps front depended upon the only tracks with solid foundations – that is Wieltje to Gravenstafel (modern maps have an 's in front of it), usable by wheeled transport up to Spree Farm; and the Potijze to Zonnebeke road as far as Frezenburg. Horses could be used for about 1500 yards beyond these points – but in any case movement beyond the limits of lorries was made considerably more difficult because of the frequency of German harassing fire. The problem had been over the previous month or so that it was almost impossible to move guns anywhere off these roads without them becoming hopelessly immersed in the mire. Thus almost all the field guns in the left sector were within a few hundred yards of Kansas Cross and on the right on Frezenburg Ridge; and the same cluttering took place for the heavy artillery, concentrated around Wieltje or just east of Potijze.

This provided several problems. Guns had been hauled into a firing position where they could find some sort of solid standing, and batteries were thereby dislocated. The existence, in effect, of only two roads with all transport requirements upon them meant that they became extraordinarily cluttered, with animals bringing up shells, with

Painting depicting the difficulties experienced in just moving artillery pieces through the Salient.

men striving to get to the front, with ambulances and men trying to bring back the wounded on stretchers, with work parties going up to the trenches, even though they were supposed to keep to duckboard tracks off the roads, and of course they were extremely vulnerable to disruption by German artillery fire and gas shells. This was so much so that the artillery were forbidden to withdraw guns for servicing and repair in this traumatic period. In addition it was also most difficult to do anything about keeping the road in some sort of repair as the routes were in such incessant use.

The effect of the gains of 4 October had been to put much of the artillery out of effective range for future operations. Attempts to push forward by field batteries had been partially successful, but this was often at the expense of battery cohesion, as guns set up where they could find a standing or where they became inextricably bogged down. The other problem was that of getting shells to these forward guns - the roads did not exist that would ensure that the task was not an almost impossible nightmare.

The Canadians were, understandably enough, to take over the guns in situ; equally understandably the gunners were highly distressed to be handing over their pristine guns in exchange for the mud locked and sorry looking specimens out on the battlefield. Matters were dismal; the officer in charge of the Corps artillery, Brigadier-General E Morrison, personally counted the artillery that he was inheriting. He should have had 250 heavy guns and 306 field guns, or 18-pounders. In fact there were only about 140 heavy guns and about 150 field guns that were serviceable and, as mentioned above, these were often scattered, some on an almost individual basis.

There was a chronic lack of 'trench stores'. Gun platforms were made of mud filled sandbags, though in due course timber rafts were constructed. Any form of shelter other than groundsheets made into a bivvy was impossible. Gun crews, as well as their weapons, were horribly exposed to enemy counter-battery fire, were often bombed and machine gunned by German aircraft and suffered frequent attacks of mustard gas. One field battery suffered two hundred percent casualties whilst serving on the Passchendaele front. Attempts to alleviate the situation were chiefly restricted to rotating the manpower as rapidly as possible, with the aim of leaving no man with the guns for more than thirty-six hours without relief.

Gunner Frank Ferguson, an American citizen, served with the 1st Canadian Siege Battery. His unit arrived in the Salient on 25 October and his diary entries in *Gunner Ferguson's Diary* provide a sardonic insight into conditions.

'*26th – My first impression of Ypres is, to say the least, not very complimentary, for as far as I can see there is not much to be seen except a lot of old bricks ands mortar, MUD, New Zealanders and more MUD. Went up to the guns this a.m. along Cambridge Road, past the famous Cloth Hall, which, by the way, was one of the things I had come over here to see, and now that it is right at my back door the darn thing hardly merits a second glance as it has been knocked to all hellangone by the Boche, and what is left is hidden by a pile of sandbags. From the billets we pass ... through St Jean, and after half an hour of swimming through the mud and trying to walk on the road dodging ASC blokes* [Army Service Corps, notorious throughout the fighting arms for being scroungers] *looking for souvenirs, we got to the guns.*'

He does not take long to sum up the situation, noting that same day,

'*The mud hereabouts is chronic; and I'll bet a cookie that every kid born in this Godforsaken neck of the woods had web toes like a duck. There is one consolation attached to being up here and that is that the "Old Man"* [the battery commander, with whom Ferguson had a stormy relationship] *won't ask us to dig him a dugout. At least not unless he wants to use it as a bathtub, as a hole dug here will fill with water almost as soon as it is dug.*'

On the 27th he came under the attention of German aircraft.

'*I heard a terrible din overhead, and looked up to see a fleet of about ten Gothas coming through the clouds dropping bombs by the ton. And to make the scene more harrowing they were heading in my direction. A machine gunner sat out on the wing of each plane sweeping the ground below, while from the bottom of the planes were dropping those lovely 'eggs' which, to my mind, are the worst things this war has brought out.*

'*I have read of people being transfixed with horror, but my mental state when looking up and seeing one of those damn things descending towards me has that phrase sounding like the 'maiden's prayer'. The only thing that brought me to my senses was a sensation of cold, and there I was up to my chest in a shell hole, said hole being full of nice cold water. I had the consolation though of seeing Colonel Ralston of the 85th* [the Nova Scotia Highlanders; actually he was a major at the time and second in command; he went on to become a Canadian Defence Minister in the Second World War] *crawling out of a mud filled gutter at the side of the road and, recognising me he remarked, "Frank, it's a tough morning", and for once in my military career I agreed with an officer.'*

A key aim of improving the transportation was to push some of the artillery further forward, not least so that it could take on some of the German artillery sheltering beyond Passchendaele. Thus three brigades of field artillery went east of the St Julien - Zonnebeke line, and six batteries of medium and heavy sized guns were brought up in their place.

The artillery plan took into account the changes in German defence tactics. In this part of the line there were not the same form of fixed defences as were usual on the Western Front. A barrage system had to be developed that could deal with machine gunners in shell holes, the pill-boxes, the wire, strongpoints in the cellars of the remains of farms and houses and the counter-attack troops that were held back behind the immediate battle line. A combination of field guns, machine-gun barrages and heavier artillery were given specific roles, providing several layers of artillery cover. The barrage was also to proceed at a much slower speed (for the first attacks, fifty yards in four minutes; in the latter phases of the battle a hundred yards in eight minutes) than was usual to take into account the difficult ground conditions under which the infantry were operating. The pill-boxes could not be tackled by the artillery except by the heaviest pieces; such artillery fire upon them would be more of a hindrance than a help because of the impact on the ground. The system of leaving these formidable obstacles to squads of soldiers was used; it had worked satisfactorily in earlier phases of Third Ypres.

The artillery was brought forward again as soon as was practicable after a successful attack. Wireless was used successfully. The reasonably good weather meant that the Royal Flying Corps were able to be used to good effect as observers and the counter-battery artillery, now much closer to the line, were able to break up the concentrations of German troops being brought up to the front. Improved roads and tramways meant that the artillery were able to harass the Germans continuously, even in the intervals between the major attacks - and this was also used as a means of confusing the enemy as to when an attack was going to take place, the fire being intensified at dawn and dusk.

Sir Douglas Haig had commented regarding earlier operations in the battle,

'There was no position which the Germans chose to hold and

fortify which our men could not take, even by frontal attack, when the guns had exercised their full power in the preparatory stages of the battle.'

The Canadian artillery lent considerable substance to this observation by its performance at Passchendaele in what was now clearly an artillery war.

The Attack of 26 October

The destruction of the banks of the Ravebeek meant that there was now an impassable area and that the attack would have to operate on **See maps pages 130 and 126** either side of it. 3rd Division was to attack on the left, with two brigades up and 4th Division would attack on the right with one brigade up.

The attack was launched at 5.40 am in mist which became steady rain; at first things went well. On the left the wire had been well cut and the two battalions of 9 Brigade (43rd and 58th Battalions) were able to make good progress towards the Red Line and captured the Bellevue pill-boxes. German artillery fire beyond this position meant that they were forced back, but they had at least secured Bellevue and got the Canadians out of the floor of the valley. This was largely due to the heroic work of Lieutenant Robert Shankland who had managed to grab some members of a Machine Gun Company and hold onto a position on the Bellevue spur to the north of the road. The grim determination of Shankland and his men meant that a reinforcing battalion (the 52nd) could take advantage of the position and consolidate and clear the area around Bellevue and fill in the gaps. This position formed part of the German Flanders I line, and although parts of it to the south had fallen some days before to the Australians, this was the first breech in it north of the Ravebeek. Shankland's bravery and dash was matched by that of Captain C O'Kelly of the 52nd Battalion who captured six pill-boxes and a hundred prisoners. Both of these men were subsequently awarded the VC, an honour that was shared by Private T Holmes of 4/CMR (Canadian Mounted Rifles). This battalion had made good progress on the extreme left of the Canadian attack, north of Wolf Farm, but had had to fall back somewhat to comply with 63rd (Royal Naval) Division on their left, which had been held up by the Germans.

On the right of the attack the 46th Battalion also started very well. The frontage of attack was more restricted on this part of the Corps front, and thus this was the sole front line battalion in the initial part of this attack. On its right was the 1st Australian Division, with the

54

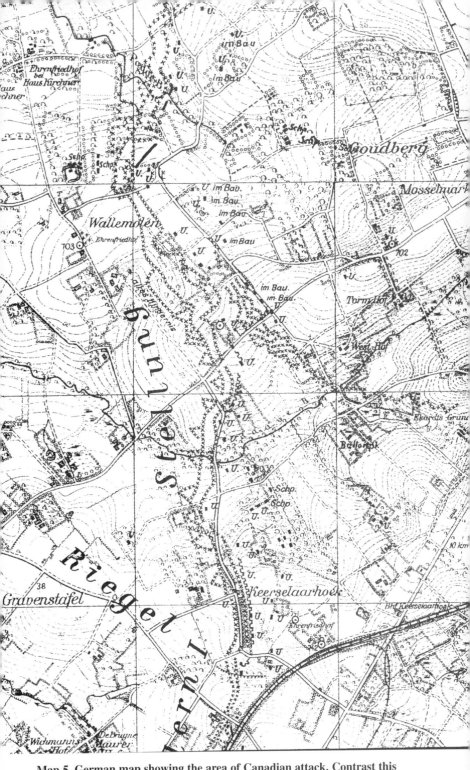

Map 5. German map showing the area of Canadian attack. Contrast this with map on pages 126 and 130.

Canadians in a communication trench during a quiet period.

boundary line between them being the railway line, exclusive to the Canadians. It did well at first, capturing all its objectives and beyond. Problems came, however, from the enfilade fire that was coming in from Laamkeek to the north and from Decline Copse, which straddled the railway.

The mistake made by the planners here was not to assign the copse to one or other of the divisions; the consequence was that neither cleared it out properly, and the Germans were thereby able to cut up the Canadians and Australians who had gone to the east of it. 46th Battalion was a weak battalion in any case, starting the attack with about 600 soldiers altogether; by the end of the day it had suffered 403 casualties. Due to confusion and the almost complete lack of landmarks the hard won ground of the battalion was gradually given up.

However, although the main attack was over, action was taken over the next couple of days to restore the situation on the right; the 46th had managed to secure enough higher and drier ground for the line to be pushed forward by the 44th (on the right) and the 47th Battalions.

The 44th (Winnipeg) Battalion had a very trying few days, commencing with their arrival in the line on 25 October, occupying the right of the divisional position. They had moved up from Van Isakers

56

Farm, a few hundred metres along on the south side of the road from the present position of Dochy Farm Cemetery. When the 46th attack went forward, the men of the 44th cleared the wounded and brought up supplies. The fall back of the 46th in front of them during the afternoon of the 26th resulted in them being stood to and some men were sent to replace the 47th who had advanced to attempt to salvage the deteriorating situation on the right flank. Battalion Headquarters were pushed forward to a pill-box, Seine dug-out, close to the railway line and in a position where communications with the front might more readily be maintained. The battalion's task was now to provide a defensive line in case of a German counter-attack and to retain stragglers who might be making their way back from the line; confusion at the front was considerable with three battalions now intermingled.

The battalion commanders involved waited for hours for firm news; at midnight a runner entered the pill-box with a message, 'Captain Lindsell of the 47th reports that he has retaken Decline Copse'. This was an illusion, a fact which was brought home to the Commanding Officer, Lieutenant-Colonel R Davies, by the arrival of a 'stalwart ANZAC officer' about two hours later. He had received the report and advanced to the copse with some scouts when he had run into a wood very much under the control of the Germans. In fact the wood that

Over the top! Canadian troops to the attack.

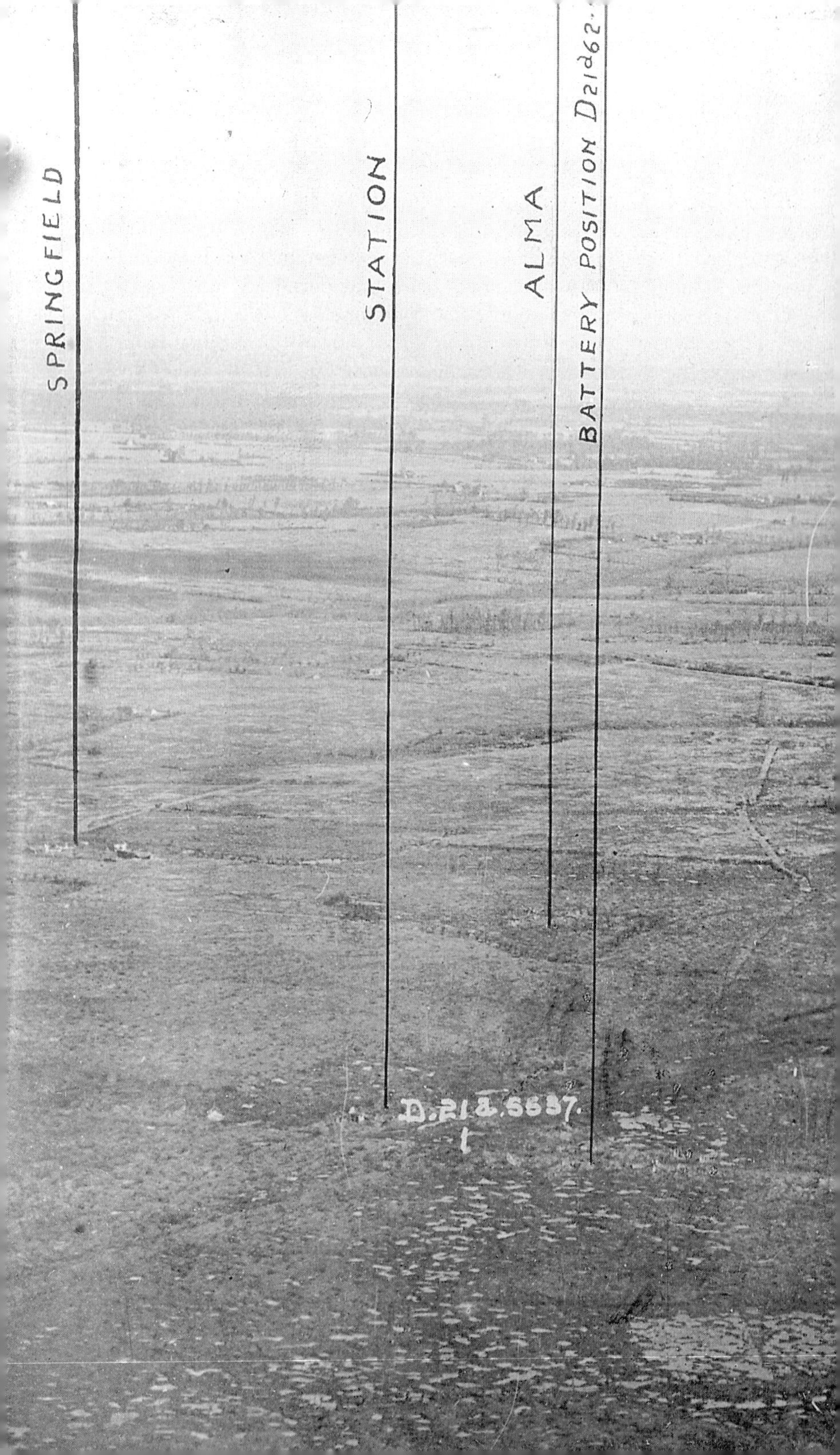

SPRINGFIELD

STATION

ALMA

BATTERY POSITION D2id62.

D.21a.5557.

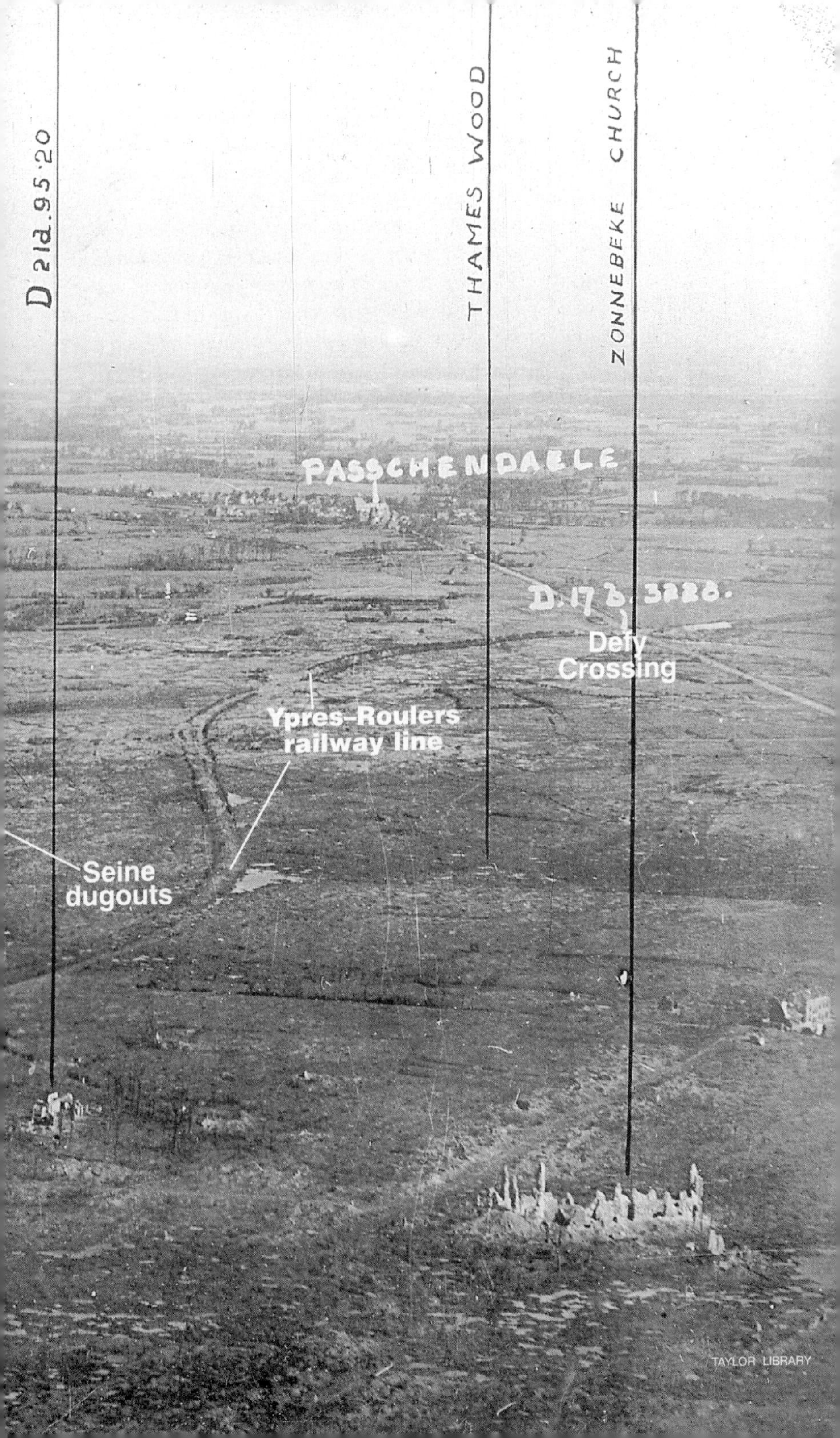

D 21d.95.20
THAMES WOOD
ZONNEBEKE CHURCH
PASSCHENDAELE
D.17 b. 3228.
Defy Crossing
Ypres–Roulers railway line
Seine dugouts
TAYLOR LIBRARY

Captain Lindsell had 'captured' was behind the original front line, a small copse on the west side of the Broodseinde road.

The confusion during the night of the 26th was considerable as is described in the 44th Regimental history.

'Stretcher bearers work doggedly in the almost hopeless task of caring for the countless wounded who mingle with the dead in the advanced positions. Parties of men lose direction in the darkness and wander to and fro in the mud, trying to find their units. The toll of killed and wounded mounts steadily under the everlasting bombardment of enemy guns. Overhead great enemy bombing planes roar back and forth. The glare of burning ammunition dumps adds to the grim terror of the scene. All night long, section by section, step by step, the men fight their way forward. Companies strive to keep intact - scarce knowing what is ahead, behind or on either flank.'

Battalion Headquarters were moved to Hamburg Crossroads, behind Dab Trench, at dawn, so that it could be in a more central position. The 47th had taken a grip of the situation to the left of the division's attack, but Decline Copse was still strongly held by the Germans. The 44th Medical Officer set up an Aid Post overnight at Hillside House, to the west of the road and in an exposed position on the western side of the ridge. By this stage the 44th had become the assault battalion as the exhausted remnants of the 46th and 50th withdrew to reserve positions to try and collect their men together and to reorganise.

The battalion gradually worked its way forward to Decline Copse, where they had to face a tremendous German bombardment, much of which consisted of gas shells.

'Officers and NCOs, compelled to discard respirators in order to carry on the work of reconnaissance, vomit frequently from the effects of the gas ...Lieutenant Jeffrey, reconnoitring close to the Copse, is shot through the head by a sniper. [He is commemorated on the Menin Gate.]

A second determined assault on Decline Copse was prepared for 10 pm; but the barrage did not hit its target but went wide. Pill-boxes in and around it were untouched, but the Canadians managed to enter the copse and close with the Germans, aided by the darkness. The strength of the German position in the copse was aided by the deep railway cutting running through it, which served to increase the confusion of any attackers.

'Lieutenant Stuart-Bailey, a newly joined officer, shot through the abdomen while leading his platoon along the railway

embankment, lies dying from his wounds, refusing to be moved until the wounded in his platoon have been cared for.' [He died of wounds at a Casualty Clearing Station near Poperinge, and is buried at Nine Elms British Cemetery.]

Eventually the Copse was captured and a line made from it to the left, to the road on the top of the ridge. Soon after 10 am the position was consolidated, and the line pushed eastwards to remove the threat provided by a number of German pill-boxes just beyond the eastern limits of Decline Copse. The position seemed secure, but the Germans were not going to allow a situation to develop whereby gains could be held in peace whilst preparations were made for a new attack. Thus on the evening of the 28th the Germans launched a sudden attack in the midst of a relief by the 85th Battalion.

'Quickly an attack is organised. Captain McKenzie, of the 85th, brings up two platoons. The 44th men, on the right along the embankment, and the 85th on the left – drive out the German troops. Two officers of the 85th are severely wounded. Lieutenant Loft of the 44th is killed [commemorated on the Menin Gate] *and another 44th officer seriously wounded. But the men press forward. Captain Martyn, leading the elements of the 44th, reaches the eastern side of the Copse alone. A party of the enemy crawls towards him. The 44th officer is in a quandary as to what to do. He calls to the 44th men behind him. Sergeant Swayne and a Lewis gun crew rush forward; only the gunner, Private Lawrence, gets through; he has his gun – but no ammunition. Corporal Hughes essays to reach the post with ammunition; he is shot through and through; with a dying effort he hurls two 'pans' forward. Pushing the officer aside, Lawrence now gets into action with his Lewis gun, mowing down the steadily advancing enemy.'*

Another gun was brought up and more men came to re-establish the line; victory had been snatched from possible defeat. What this account shows is how 'small' and seemingly insignificant actions by an individual or a small group of men provide often the turning point in a particular battle.

The regimental history makes one final note: 'Before leaving the battlefield the 44th buries its dead, a custom always followed by the unit – but one that is extremely difficult in the gruesome conditions at Passchendaele.' Alas, this was largely in vain, as the majority of the graves were blown up and lost in later fighting.

The battalion escaped relatively lightly at Passchendaele – with sixty seven men killed, although a disproportionate number of them were officers and NCOs. The history records, in an uncharacteristic note:

> 'With all its horrors, Passchendaele brings a deep sense of satisfaction to the men of the 44th'

The attack of the 26th had turned out in the end to be quite successful - even though it took longer - far longer - than was anticipated to hold and consolidate a position which was close to the original objective, one which was fully achieved only (eventually) on the right of the attack.

The attack had also been one of great heroism, best indicated, perhaps, by the award of the three Victoria Crosses mentioned earlier. All of these were won by men who were fighting to the north of the Gravenstafel – Mosselmarkt road. The first of them was won by Lieutenant Robert Shankland, who had already won the DCM as an RSM in August 1916. His VC citation reads:

R Shankland
VC

> 'For most conspicuous bravery and resource in action under critical and adverse conditions. Having gained a position he rallied the remnant of his own platoon and men of other companies, disposed them to command the ground in front, and inflicted heavy casualties upon the retreating enemy. Later, he dispersed a counter-attack, thus enabling supporting troops to come up unmolested. He then personally communicated to Headquarters an accurate and valuable report as to the position on the brigade frontage and, after doing so, rejoined his command and carried on until relieved. His courage and splendid example inspired all ranks and, coupled with his great gallantry and skill, undoubtedly saved a very critical situation.'

VC citations are not usually very specific about the location of the action where the deed took place. Lieutenant Shankland was a member of the 43rd Battalion, which was attacking immediately to the north of the Bellevue Road; both sides of the attack in this area were suffering considerable damage from the German pill-boxes on the crest and flanks of the hill on which this tiny hamlet sat. The Germans considered the Bellevue spur to be the key to Passchendaele, a proposition with which it is difficult to disagree once the ground has been examined. Shankland and a small group of men made it to the crest of the hill and removed the offending pill-boxes. However his numbers were severely depleted, whilst on the right the 58th Battalion was in considerable difficulties, in particular from machine guns situated in Snipe Hall and numbers of men, largely officerless, were falling back to their original start line. Shankland held his position despite heavy artillery, machine gun and infantry attacks. *Thirty Canadian VCs* described the situation thus:

'*At no time previously had our men experienced such shelling. The mud and water dispersed by the busting shells clogged the weapons of the Canadians and, in spite of instant attention, rendered many of them temporarily useless. The going was terribly hard but* [he] *held his battered line for four hours along the crest of the spur, keeping his men together and in good spirits, recruiting those soldiers of other companies who had gained the hill but were left without officers, and maintaining against heavy counter-attack the Canadian position that had cost so much to win.*'

The decision to return to Headquarters and brief the senior officers was a vital contribution to the success of the day's operation, as without it there was only the haziest and incoherent notion of what was going on, which hampered support fire from the artillery and the heavy machine guns. Orders could now be given to supporting infantry and to the artillery to take action to rectify the situation, so that what might have been another dismal failure was transformed into a relative success, even if the line gained was not as far as had been hoped.

Shankland was thirty when he gained his VC; he had emigrated to Canada (to Winnipeg) from Ayr, where he had been a clerk at the railway station. His job in Canada was not much more glamorous, being an assistant cashier in a creamery! He enlisted soon after the war began, went through all the non commissioned ranks and ended his war as a Lieutenant-Colonel. He died in 1968 in Vancouver, just after the fiftieth anniversary of his VC being gazetted.

Captain Christopher O'Kelly won his VC whilst serving with the 52nd Battalion, not far from where Lieutenant Shankland gained his. The citation reads:

'*For most conspicuous bravery in an action in which he led his company with extraordinary skill and determination. After the original attack had failed and two companies of his unit had launched a new attack, Captain O'Kelly advanced his command over a thousand yards under heavy fire without any artillery barrage, took the enemy positions on the crest of the hill by storm and then personally organised and led a series of attacks against pill-boxes, his company alone capturing six of them, with a hundred prisoners and ten machine guns. Later on in the afternoon, under the leadership of this gallant officer, his*

C P J O'Kelly

company repelled a strong counter-attack, taking more prisoners, and subsequently during the night captured a hostile raiding party consisting of one officer, ten men and a machine gun.'

This action was directly linked with that of Lieutenant Shankland. O'Kelly's company was ordered forward to hold the left flank of Shankland's very exposed position. *Thirty Canadian VCs* rather quaintly describes the attitude of the men at this time, 'drenched by the steady rain and pounded by the enemy's shells, the men of the 52nd were very bored indeed with inaction.' They managed to advance quickly and effectively, catching a lot of Germans in the flank as they gained the brow of the hill. Pill-boxes were put out of action by the tried and established method of small parties creeping up to them whilst their fellows covered all the loop holes and entrances with rifle grenades and heavy fire. Once the small attacking group got into the dead ground (ie out of the line of fire of the defenders) by the apertures, they would throw in a grenade, which in the enclosed space of these concrete fortifications had a devastating and utterly demoralising effect. The Germans were able to regroup to some extent in the ruins of Bellevue Farm, and there was considerable fierce fighting in the outhouses and other remnants of the building. In due course, once a new line was established, the men of his company (A) and B that had come up in support were able to fight off German counter-attacks and indeed during the night he launched a number of raids to dislocate the Germans before they could reorganise themselves in anticipation of a further advance.

O'Kelly subsequently became a major; he died in 1922, shortly after the end of the war, in Ontario.

Over to the left of the attack Thomas Holmes, a nineteen year old private of the 4th Canadian Mounted Rifles, won a VC in the vicinity of Wolf Farm and Wolf Copse. His citation reads:

T W Holmes

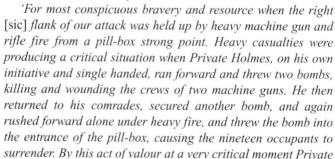

'For most conspicuous bravery and resource when the right [sic] flank of our attack was held up by heavy machine gun and rifle fire from a pill-box strong point. Heavy casualties were producing a critical situation when Private Holmes, on his own initiative and single handed, ran forward and threw two bombs, killing and wounding the crews of two machine guns. He then returned to his comrades, secured another bomb, and again rushed forward alone under heavy fire, and threw the bomb into the entrance of the pill-box, causing the nineteen occupants to surrender. By this act of valour at a very critical moment Private

Berlin Wood ——— Marsh Bottom ———

Marsh Bottom with Abraham Heights and Gravenstafel on the horizon.

Holmes undoubtedly cleared the way for the advance of our troops and saved the lives of many of his comrades.'

4/CMR was on the extreme left of the Canadian attack, with Hood Battalion of 63rd (Royal Naval) Division on their left. The objective of the battalion was to capture Woodland Copse and Source Farm, with the aim of creating a new jumping off position along Wallemolen Ridge for the final assault upon Passchendaele. The main problem the battalion had to endure was the sitting in the jumping-off trenches under persistent and searching German fire before the attack was launched in the early hours of the 26th. The effective artillery barrage had removed much of the protective fire in front of the pill-boxes, and although they kept up a persistent harassing machine-gun fire, they were generally cleared without causing major hold-ups. However the closer that the attackers came to the main Flanders I Line the harder the progress became and in particular in front of Wolf Copse.

'North-east of Wolf Copse a German pill-box was situated, its own strong defences supplemented by a machine gun mounted close to the building on each side, and against their fire our men advanced, at times up to their waists in water. It was not possible to advance quickly, and man after man of our small attacking force went down into the mud. Reinforcements from A Company came up on the right, and a series of gallant attempts were made to rush the enemy's position, which was holding up our entire local advance. Each time our men failed to get home, and eventually they were forced to take whatever cover was possible some fifty yards from the pill-box.'

It was at this stage in proceedings that Private Holmes carried out his extraordinary acts of bravery, and which allowed for the relative success of the Canadian attack on this part of the front.

The Canadian casualties of the attack of 26th October and the two subsequent days of consolidation, came to 2481; about 1600 were suffered on the first day, of whom 585 were killed. These casualties of course include all those many that were suffered in the gun lines, by the medical teams, by the men bringing up the rations, shells, ammunition and trench supplies and by those maintaining the roads, mule tracks and light railways.

The British had now to set about the next in this phase of attacks; and once more the Canadians were to play a vital part.

Canadian troops coming out of the line after the battle in October 1917.

Chapter Four

THE TAKING OF CREST FARM, MEETCHEELE
AND SOURCE FARM
The attack of 30 October

The advance had brought the inevitable problem about supply; the comparative lull of a few days allowed the Engineers and Pioneers, with additional labour from the infantry, to get on with the vital task of ensuring a mule track was constructed within each brigade area. These were made from planks, half logs of wood wired firmly together (known as corduroy because of the rippled surface) and given depth by the use of fascines, ie bundles of branches tied firmly together to provide a firm whole. These tracks were designed so that the mule trains could bring up all the necessary trench stores and ammunition for the next phase of the attack; the infantry had to make do with rather inferior offerings, or at worst travel as best they could across the quagmire.

The next attack was to capture a line from below Vienna Cottage (near the Ypres-Roulers railway), where the Corps was alongside the Australians, to Vapour Farm, north west of Passchendaele. Here the Corps was on the extreme left of Second Army, and their neighbours were 63rd (Royal Naval) Division, the right of Fifth Army.

The battle was launched in the early hours of 30 October, at 5.50 am when, seemingly for once, it was not raining. The attack on the right, which will be described more fully later, went well, though an early entry into an almost empty Passchendaele had to be abandoned because of difficulties on the left; the line was bent back along the morass of the Ravebeek valley.

On the extreme left good progress was also made, but the 63rd Division, in lower and swampier ground, had great difficulty in making progress. However Source Farm was taken and held by sheer grit and determination; Furst Farm was captured and the swampy ground between the two, in the vicinity of Woodland Plantation, was to be held by patrols. The gains of a thousand yards or so along a front of a mile-and-a-half were impressive.

85th Battalion (Nova Scotia Highlanders) CEF
This battalion placed a memorial on its battlefield here at

See map
on page
130 Passchendaele before the end of the war. It survives to this day, somewhat awkwardly. It is a small cenotaph placed near the limit of its advance on this day, not far short of the final line achieved during the battle for Passchendaele. It is awkward because of the difficulty of modern access – ie there is no really safe car-parking, and the immaculate lawn path out to it must, to put it mildly, be trying for the local farmer. Yet it is moving – uniquely so, perhaps, for the Canadians, not only because of its significant position for the battalion but also because on it are recorded the names of 135 Other Ranks and 13 officers who fell in the days of this battle. To my mind it is the most poignant of the Passchendaele memorials.

The 85th had been in billets at Brandhoek, a small hamlet on the Vlamertinge to Poperinge road; by this stage in the war the fields all around and about had been transformed into great hutted encampments, supply dumps, Casualty Clearing Stations (it was here that Captain Noel Chavasse died of wounds received in action that were to bring a bar to his Victoria Cross), horse lines and even major railway sidings. They made their way to the line via Potijze and the Zonnebeke Road, '...which was congested to the utmost with army vehicles of every description and moving artillery, pack mule trains, and troops of every arm of the service.'[1] They then went along a track which was only wide enough to allow them to proceed single file; though difficult it was better than being on the road at this stage. 'Often salvoes of incendiary bombs would land on the road and illuminate the country for miles around and scurrying men and stampeded mules and disorganised traffic could plainly be seen.'

The idea was that the men would be in the line for a day before they went over the top, arriving on the evening of 28 October. As D Company was going into the line to relieve the 44th Battalion, the Germans launched a counter-attack in the area of Decline Copse, as described in the last chapter. Immediately the Company Commander, Captain MacKenzie, launched his men into a counter-attack; the sudden impact of these new arrivals threw the Germans into confusion and they withdrew. However, German snipers and machine gunners had taken a heavy toll, including MacKenzie, who was mortally wounded in the stomach. Despite this wound he went on with the company and reorganised the line before allowing himself to be put on a stretcher, dying soon afterwards. All the other company officers were killed as well; the only one who has a known grave is Lieutenant Norman Christie who was wounded but killed by a shell whilst awaiting treatment.

D Company remained holding the line throughout the 29th, having to keep a very low profile in the inadequate shell holes and shallow trench that passed for the front line. The Germans in some instances were very close, only twenty yards or so away. As night fell the three attacking companies moved up and replaced D Company; before the barrage fell the attackers fell back to allow the artillery to work on the Germans, a necessary move because of the proximity of the positions. However, the barrage seemed to have been largely ineffectual, despite its awesome sound.

'Zero hour was preceded with its usual period of quiet when at the grey dawn one small gun in the rear boomed out. This seemed to be the signal, for instantly every possible kind of gun belched forth its fire and shells, eighteen-ponders, machine guns, howitzers and heavies sending their whizzing missiles overhead to the enemy lines beyond.'

The main problems were once again on the right and reserve platoons had to be brought forward to assist and help in the removal of machine

At night a busy piece of roadway in the Salient, but the Germans knew it and sent shells over regularly on predetermined coordinates, almost inevitably finding a target. TAYLOR LIBRARY

Area of Decline Copse

85th Battalion memorial. The railway line's course is marked by the line of bushes and trees.

gun posts and small pill-boxes. Quite quickly the situation was resolved and the Germans beat a rapid and hasty retreat.

> 'As the resistance slackened our men with a loud cheer rushed upon them with the bayonet and soon dispatched those who had not escaped in precipitate flight. Amidst all the fearfulness of the situation our boys were able to see the humour in the mad flight of the Hun.
>
> 'Captain Campbell with the aid of rifle grenades promptly captured two machine guns. A Lewis gun section had already captured another and had it trained on the fleeing Boche who were seen dropping in all directions before a shower of bullets 'made in Germany'. By the time the objective was taken six German machine guns had been captured, one whizz bang and field guns, but only six prisoners, two of whom were wounded, and the other four were needed to carry our wounded.'

This is an unusually emotive account for a unit history; the author had served with the Battalion (he was the medical officer) and it is quite clear that he was an 'angry young man' with his blood still up when he wrote this particular account. He went on to win the DSO in 1918.

The vital time after an initially successful attack is the moments immediately afterwards – consolidation is essential, especially when facing such a formidable opponent as the Germans. Captain Campbell was in charge of the right flank.

> 'He was proceeding through the line with his inevitable Lewis gun, with which he was an expert, when a shell landed close to him and knocked him and his gun into a shell hole. After he had daubed some iodine on his wounded face from his field dressing

From here the British could look over the German Lines for the first time for three years.

and got the blood stopped he scrambled out of the shell hole and went to his task again. On returning he found that Major Anderson (adjutant and in charge of the left flank) had been killed an hour after they had parted and that there were only three subalterns [ie junior officers] *left in the whole battalion in the front lines.'*

He took control of the battle, placing his battle headquarters towards the centre of the line (not far from the site of the monument) putting there two Lewis gun positions to cover his flanks. The following morning the Germans put down a terrific barrage on the thinly held line, and launched yet another counter attack upon the sorely tried men. Major Ralston, the second in command (he who had a close encounter with a German bomb near Gunner Ferguson), had organised a new company the previous night, which consisted of, 'bandsmen, cooks, orderlies, batmen, hostlers, shoemakers, tailors, blacksmiths as well as the NCOs and men who had been left out as a nucleus for reorganisation, and every man who was at hand.' These men and their invaluable Lewis guns arrived in the line just in time to assist with the quelling of the German counter-attack. Eventually the battalion was relieved during the night of 31 October, reaching their transport lines at Potijze at daybreak.

The Capture of Crest Farm: 72nd (Seaforth Highlanders of Canada) Battalion CEF

The battalion came into the line, as did the 85th, on the night of 28 October; it had one company take over the line, one in support at Hillside Farm and two at Abraham Heights, the latter in relative See map on page 126

71

An aerial view over the Canadian attacks taken on 17 October 1917. The ravaged ground is clearly portrayed.

AUGUSTUS WOOD

HENDAELE.

17.10.17.

PASSCHENDAELE - ZONNEBEKE ROAD.

security. The reconnaissance of the ground over which the attack was to be launched revealed a nasty surprise; Haalen Copse was either under water or a swampy quagmire, and quite impassable. A radical change in plan had to be ordered, a not inconsiderable feat given the late hour and the necessity to ensure that higher formations and the artillery were fully conversant with what was now to take place.

The battalion would now have to set off, as planned, but then would have to bunch up to negotiate a gap only fifty yards wide before the attacking companies could spread out once more into waves. To distract the enemy, the four Vickers machine guns, together with the Stokes mortar teams and four Lewis guns were to concentrate their fire on the rear of Haalen Copse and on the south western approaches to Crest Farm, the battalion objective.

During the night D Company had cleared Deck Wood of Germans (although twelve emerged from an old trench that had been overlooked – they surrendered very rapidly once the advance began) and the remaining companies followed on the very effective barrage with their right flank on the minor road which passes through the west side of Passchendaele.

Crest Farm was proving to be every bit as difficult to overcome as anticipated, but A Company managed to get on to the higher ground to the west of the position and, in conjunction with the rest of the attacking force, almost encircled the position. It captured twenty five men and four machine guns and killed fifty. It then proceeded to move north, with the intention of joining up with the men of the PPCLI. In the process they captured more machine guns, using some of them against the retreating Germans, and then began to consolidate their position.

B Company went in a more northerly direction, and fought its way to the high point of the farm, killing forty and capturing thirty Germans, as well as three machine guns. The most notable deed of a member of this company was the action of Lance Corporal Irwin, in charge of a Lewis gun. He discovered three German machine guns in position on the crest, which had not yet opened fire, but which were all trained on A Company and were ready to enfilade them.

'With a bravery that was tinged with the uncanny prescience of an Indian scout, he worked in behind the fated Boche gunners and, firing his Lewis gun from the shoulder, killed every member of the crews who were just going to begin to fire, and captured the three guns single-handed. One of the latter was immediately trained on the enemy.'[2]

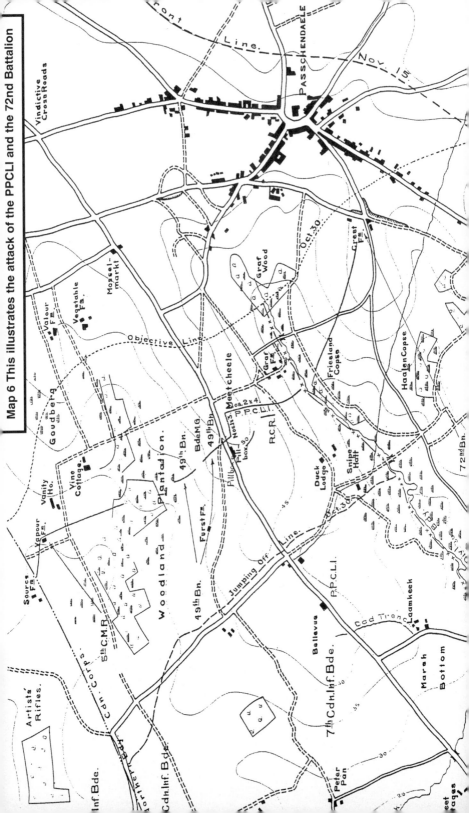

Map 6 This illustrates the attack of the PPCLI and the 72nd Battalion

C Company kept to the right of the attack, with one platoon firmly on the battalion boundary. One of the platoons aided the storming of Crest Farm by attacking it from the east side. Others moved forward so that they controlled all the north west approaches to the village and assisted in the encirclement of the Crest Farm position and the removal of the remaining German defenders. At this point patrols were sent in to the main part of the village, which the Germans seemed to be evacuating.

The success of the attack was largely due to the closeness with which the men followed the barrage, a risky business given that artillery fire, especially given the condition of the guns, often 'dropped short' of its target. The attack had actually resulted in relatively few casualties though,

> 'it had been an operation fraught with every chance of disaster. The machine-gun officer of the German battalion that had held the position said, on being captured, that he had no fewer than twenty-four machine guns defending the front attacked – about 500 yards. Twelve of these guns were massed on the knoll of the farm itself. "But," he said in perfect English, "your men attacked so closely upon the barrage that they seemed to be mixed up with their own shell fire! My guns had no time to come properly into action".'

Haig commented in part of his despatch that, 'the unit which took Crest Farm had by this action accomplished a feat of arms which would go down in the annals of British history as one of the greatest achievements of a single unit'. Indeed even to-day, with the encroachment of housing to the south, it is quite clear what a dominating position the farm had over the spurs which came off south

Crest Farm lies beyond the houses. View from SSE of Crest Farm on road towards Tyne Cot. Arrows indicate line of attack.

Boardwalk weaving through craters connecting captured pill-boxes. TAYLOR LIBRARY

westwards from the main ridge. It is a fitting place for the Canadian Memorial to this battle.

The 72nd (known as the Kilties) remained in their newly won position until they were relieved in the early hours of 2 November. Their relatively light casualty list was inflated by very heavy German artillery fire and several counter-attacks to 280 men.

Princess Patricia's Canadian L I – and two Victoria Crosses

The PPCLI was an unusual unit, founded at the beginning of the war by a quite extraordinary man, Hamilton Gault, whose biography has recently been published.[3] This regiment at its foundation had a representative from all but one regiment of the British army when it was first recruited; it is now one of the few surviving regular infantry regiments in the Canadian army.

On 16 October it moved north from the Vimy area towards the Salient, enjoying a week or so in the rear area during which time it worked hard on physical fitness and brushing up basic skills. Parties of men were sent up every day to have a look at the line whilst the Second Army model, created by the Army Topographical section, of the Passchendaele area was examined closely by all ranks. This was of a similar type to that produced in the open for that Army's attack on Messines. This one was housed in a vast hangar 400 x 150 feet; the model showed trees, roads, pill-boxes and so forth and was corrected every day from the evidence provided by aerial photography.

The battalion had a particularly intractable problem to face even before it could begin the attack proper – a problem whose solution was vital to the whole of this phase of the Canadian attack. That problem was Snipe Hall. All attempts to remove this obstacle in the time since the attack of 26 October had failed, protected as it was by the marshy ground before and around it, and from enfilade fire from both sides of the Ravebeek valley. The decision was made to capture the position by night attack; despite the obstacles, small trenches, the difficulties of the muddy ground, operating in a new area and under machine-gun fire, the position was carried before daybreak and the line was straightened. Contact of sorts could now be made with the neighbouring 72nd Battalion, though this was soon lost once the attack commenced.

> *'The Ravebeek, which separated the two divisions, was three-and-a-half to four feet deep; its bottom was marshy, its banks had been shot away by the artillery, and the ground on both sides, from Snipe Hall through Friesland Copse to Graf Wood, was a swamp impassable for attacking troops.'*[4]

The Regimental history makes a number of apposite points. Unlike the attack at Vimy, only six months or so earlier, it was quite impossible in the conditions to give specific battle orders; the CO commented, 'it was quite useless to lay down any mode of attack to troops going over unknown and swamped lands, pitted with shell holes filled with water'. Indeed the Divisional commander, Major-General Louis Lipsett had made plain in his orders that there was little a commanding officer could do beyond arranging the disposition of his companies and that, 'NCOs are to be impressed that in this operation success or failure will more than ever depend upon their initiative and resource'. Because of the ground conditions it was decided to go against the normal practice of using the intermediate objective line as a point at which the supporting companies would leapfrog through the initial attackers; instead these latter would carry out this task and mop up strong points and pill-boxes; the front line companies were to press on to the final objective. The conditions also meant that the troops carried more than might be expected – 170 extra rounds of ammunition, a muzzle-protector for the rifle (this to prevent the barrel being clogged with mud and therefore potentially lethal for the firer), an aeroplane flare, three days' rations, sandbags and a shovel. Finally, the artillery barrage was to lift at a very slow rate – fifty yards every four minutes or 750 yards an hour which 'must surely be the low record for a charge in all the history of warfare'. The CO, Agar Adamson, deemed it to be the right speed because of the ground conditions.

The proximity of the trenches meant that the troops withdrew a good hundred yards from their front line positions for the opening barrage. The attack was launched - or, rather, wallowed - and immediately came under heavy fire from Duck Lodge and Graf Farm before them and Meetcheele Ridge and the pill-box there. Within an hour or so most of the officers were casualties, as were more than thirty of the more senior NCOs. The 49th Battalion made good progress and got to Furst Farm, on the northern side of the ridge; but the PPCLI continued to be held up by Duck Lodge. Communications broke down and were dependent upon runners, who brought back to the report centre at the Bellevue pill-box messages on 1:10000 map report forms.

On the right of the attack the hold-up was caused by isolated groups of Germans, equipped with rifles and light machine guns who had to be removed by flank attacks; and this laborious and man-consuming process had to be continued right up to and including Duck Lodge itself. The intermediate objective now gained, there was time to reorganise and marshal the remnants of the battalion for the attack in fifty or so minutes the attacking force of 600 had been reduced to two weak companies.

The 49th Battalion were unable to make much further headway, having suffered considerably from machine-gun fire from the Meetcheele pill-box; they were able to keep touch with the left of the PPCLI and to patrol out to the swampland of Woodland Plantation, but were in no fit state to assist materially with a further advance – indeed they were quite dependent on 7 Brigade Machine Gun Company (7/MGC) to help them retain the position that they had gained. In the course of the fighting Private Cecil Kinross of the 49th (Alberta) Battalion won the VC.

'For most conspicuous bravery in action during prolonged and severe operations. Shortly after the attack was launched, the company to which he belonged came under intense artillery fire, and further advance was held up by a very severe fire from an enemy machine gun. Private Kinross, making a careful survey of the situation, deliberately divested himself of all his equipment save his rifle and bandolier and, regardless of his personal

C J Kinross
VC

79

Graf Farm   Graf Wood   Meetcheele

View from Crest Farm to north west. Note the valley which was impassible for the attacking troops.

safety, advanced alone over the open ground in broad daylight, charged the enemy machine gun, killing the crew of six, and seized and destroyed the gun. His superb example and courage instilled the greatest confidence in his company, and enabled a further advance of three hundred yards to be made and a highly important position to be established. Throughout the day he showed marvellous coolness and courage, fighting with the utmost aggressiveness against heavy odds until severely wounded'

A Scotsman by birth, whose family had emigrated to Alberta, this brave man survived his wounds and lived for another forty years.

As usual, the VC citation is very coy about where all this took place, even though the fighting was well and truly over by the time the gazette announcing the award was published in January 1918. The machine gun mentioned in the citation was near Furst Farm; its field of fire covered the attack by the battalion and threatened to bring the advance to a premature halt, the losses up to this point already being significant. The heavy ground, the German artillery fire and the need to deal with the various strong points and isolated machine guns had already caused the impetus of the advance to stumble. Kinross' action ensured that the advance could continue, but by the time that the intermediate objective was reached the attacking force had been reduced to a mere four officers and 125 men. Thus the intervention of the Machine Gun Company was vital to hold the position; and the precariousness of it was only relieved by the arrival of reinforcements from the Royal Canadian Regiment.

The PPCLI left had suffered considerable losses in their advance up the ridge, and the position seemed desperate when they came before the pill-box on the crest, which continued to deal out death from its loop holes. Here took place that relatively rare occurrence even amongst the unusual cases when VCs were won – for what followed was an action which brought two VCs.

Briefly what happened was that a flanking attack was attempted on the pill-box; Lieutenant Christie took up a position on the left, and used his skills as a battalion sniper to try and keep the Germans' heads down; meanwhile Lieutenant McKenzie (MacKenzie on his citation) 7/MGC led a charge on the pill-box, having reorganised the men, in the course of which he was killed. This puts it somewhat baldly: he had also sent details off to deal with the scattered German outposts that continued to provide deadly fire; he attempted to get some men around to the rear; and he finally arranged two parties to make the attack, from different angles, in the course of which he was killed. His citation reads,

'For most conspicuous bravery and leading when in charge of a section of four machine guns accompanying the infantry in an attack. Seeing that all of the officers and most of the NCOs of an infantry company had become casualties and that the men were hesitating before a nest of enemy machine guns, which were on commanding ground and causing them severe casualties, he handed over command of his guns to an NCO, rallied the infantry, organised an attack and captured the strong point. Finding that the strong point was swept by machine-gun fire from a pill-box which dominated all the ground over which the troops were advancing, Lieutenant MacKenzie made a reconnaissance and detailed flanking and frontal attacking parties which captured the pill-box, he himself being killed while leading the frontal attack. By his valour and leadership this gallant officer ensured the capture of these strong points and so saved the lives of many men.'

**H McKenzie
VC**

The VC is counted by the PPCLI as being one of theirs, for it was done in company with the battalion and he had served with them until he was commissioned in early 1917. McKenzie is commemorated on the Menin Gate.

The other VC was won by the then Sergeant George Mullin, a regimental sniper; he was born in the USA but moved to Canada at an early age and died there in 1963. He was one of the flanking party, and whilst the frontal attacks distracted the defenders, he took prompt action,

G H Mullin VC

'For most conspicuous bravery in attack when, single handed, he captured a commanding pill-box which had withstood the heavy bombardment and was causing heavy casualties to our forces and holding up the attack. He rushed a sniper's post in front, destroyed the garrison with bombs and, crawling on top of the pill-box, he shot the two machine gunners with his revolver. He then rushed to another entrance and compelled the garrison of ten to surrender. His gallantry and fearlessness were witnessed by many, and although rapid fire was directed upon him and his clothes riddled by bullets, he never faltered in his purpose, and he not only helped to save the situation but also indirectly saved many lives.'

It was impossible to make much further progress, especially as the Germans still had strong points just above and below Graf Farm, and in any case numbers were severely depleted. The Germans launched several counter-attacks, mainly from the left, as with the loss of Crest Farm the other side of the valley was not a practicable possibility. Their attack line stretched from Vindictive cross roads to Venture Farm, but these attacks were broken up by the artillery and machine-gun fire. Still, the battalion was reduced to about 250 men to hold a difficult and (especially at the crest) exposed front and reinforcements were sent up from the supporting battalion, the Royal Canadian Regiment. Eventually a line was consolidated from the Graf Farm road to Furst Farm, but by that evening the battalion was down to 180 men. After another day in the line the battalion was withdrawn during the evening of 31 October and by the early hours of the 1st they had made their way back to Pommern Castle.

Their part in the attack (though not in this part of the Salient) was now complete; the battalion only lost similarly heavily at Sanctuary Wood in 1916 and at Tilloy in September 1918. 363 were casualties out of the 600 who went into action; twenty of the twenty five officers (nine died), 343 Other Ranks, including 150 who were killed or missing, believed killed. In total, 750 PPCLI were killed in the Salient in the Great War, and their battalion memorial stands on the ridge above Bellewaarde, where they had fought in the Second Battle of Ypres in the spring of 1915.

Major Pearkes' (5th Canadian Mounted Rifles) Victoria Cross

This man not only won the VC but in the course of the war also the DSO and MC and was wounded five times. He remained in the army after the armistice, commanded the 1st (Canadian) Division in 1940, commanded Pacific Command 1942 - 1945, became Canadian Defence Minister between 1957 and 1960 and was Lieutenant-Governor of British Columbia 1963 - 1967. This brave and accomplished man was born at Watford in 1888 and died in 1986, just short of his 98th birthday.

His story as told by *Thirty Canadian VCs*[5] tells what happened, as well, on the left of the Canadian attack.

He was a member of 5th Canadian Mounted Rifles, the lead battalion on 8 Brigade front. They were launched upon Vapour Farm and the north western defences of Passchendaele. The ground before them was very difficult and it was considered impracticable to traverse Woodland Plantation - one company was sent to the north, another to the south. Their initial progress was screened from the Germans in the Plantation by the use of smoke. A runner reported to Battalion HQ that the left hand company had gained their intermediate objective but that,

> '*On the right the men of A Company had encountered the enemy south of the wood and fierce hand-to-hand fighting was going on, with the Canadians steadily making their way forward. In this bayonet work, with their opponents waist-deep in mud and water, our men won the advantage, for the knowledge that a misstep or a disabling wound meant a peculiarly unpleasant death in suffocating mud was an incentive to desperate fighting, and the Germans hated it from the start.*'

The two leading companies had suffered about fifty percent casualties and had, not surprisingly, become disorganised in the heavy initial fighting. They managed to meet up on the far side of the plantation and stopped to rest whilst the artillery continued their bombardment of the intermediate objective; this was a mistake as it gave the Germans time to reorganise and they began to open effective fire from the east, around Vanity Farm and Goudberg. Major Pearkes took over command and led his men onwards, out of sight of his battalion headquarters; about half an hour after he set off he reported that he had got through to his final objective with about fifty men remaining.

> '*He had taken his men forward, fighting his way through obstacle after obstacle, and now he was holding a hastily improvised line with both his flanks exposed to any German attack. On his left the Artists Rifles* [of 63rd (Royal Naval) Division] *had been unable to capture Source Farm, and from this point heavy enfilading fire was being poured upon his exposed line.*'

Pearkes realised that the only hope of improving the situation would be

G R Pearkes VC

by storming Source Farm, which he proceeded to do by the sheer guts and determination of his troops and then proceeded, extraordinarily enough, to proceed with his advance. As it became increasingly clear that the rest of the attack on either flank was going to come nowhere near his gains, he withdrew from Vanity Farm and settled his men into positions between Source and Vapour farms, preparing to meet counter-attacks with the grand total of twenty men. The position was not only under fire from the front, but the ground over which they had come was now swept by enemy machine-gun fire, and the men sent up to support his pitifully small band (from 2/CMR) suffered very heavy casualties as they made their way across the swampy morass. So out on a limb was his position that it was seriously considered that it should be given up, but it was reasoned, and the Corps Commander, Lieutenant-General Currie, agreed, that as the ground would have to be won again in the next phase of the operation that it should be retained, whatever the difficulties.

At the end of such an exhausting day's work it was only just that Pearkes should win the greatest award for outstanding bravery and courage that the King Emperor could bestow.

The battle had gone quite well, viewed from the perspective of the higher formations; although the ground remained treacherous and boggy on the left of the attack, a much firmer launch pad had at long last been reached on the right; the situation was favourable for a direct attack on the brick stained mud that was all that remained of Passchendaele.

1 *The 85th in France and Flanders* J. Hayes. Further descriptions of the 85th come from this source.

2 *History of 72nd Battalion Canadian Expeditionary Force, Seaforth Highlanders of Canada* B McEvoy and Captain Abraham Heights Finlay

3 *First in the Field: Gault of the Patricias* Jeffery Williams, Leo Cooper 1995

4 Much of the information in this chapter comes from the excellent PPCLI Regimental History: *Princess Patricia's Canadian Light Infantry 1914-1919*, R Hodder-Williams

5 *Thirty Canadian VCs*, Captain J Roberts, Skeffington

View from below Crest Farm looking towards Passchendaele Ridge, a dreary landscape even today.

Chapter Five

THE FALL OF PASSCHENDAELE AND THE END OF THE THIRD BATTLE OF YPRES

With the bulk of the defending ridges seized and the high and firmer ground to the south firmly in Canadian hands the time had come to launch the assault on Passchendaele. Currie replaced the two Canadian divisions in the line with the 1st and the 2nd, which took up their positions during the night of 4 November. Currie's plan was to take Passchendaele (2nd Division) and Mosselmarkt and Goudberg (1st Division) in the first phase, launched on 6 November and the second phase would take place on 10 November to extend the line along the ridge to the north and would take the area around Vindictive Cross Roads and Hill 52, the high point of the ridge on the road to Westroosebeke.

The Germans had also carried out a relief, removing the shattered 39th Division. This had had a good record at the Somme, but not done so well at the latter stages of the Battle of Verdun in the fighting of December; however it was rested and re-equipped with good quality conscripts and had performed creditably under the most trying of conditions; its replacement was the 11th Division, which had only arrived from the Champagne on 3 November. This Formation had a good fighting record, although the presence of a number of Poles in its ranks, not particularly keen to fight for Germany, was considered a weakness. It was this division that was given the task of hanging on to Passchendaele until the weather finally forced the British to give up their attack.

The left of the divisional attack suffered from the familiar problem of struggling through the morass of the Ravebeek valley before they could get to grips with the enemy. Graf Farm remained a thorn in the side of the attack whilst low flying German aircraft strafed the struggling infantry. This did have a faintly amusing side to it, as Nicholson reports: 'One ground target that received particular attention during the attack was the start line of the 31st Battalion [to the north of Crest Farm], where German airmen mistook a row of greatcoats for troops.'[1]

Passchendaele was entered by the 27th (City of Winnipeg) Battalion and it was here that Private James Peter Robertson won his Victoria Cross.

**J P
Robertson
VC**

'For most conspicuous bravery and outstanding devotion to duty in attack. When his platoon was held up by uncut wire and a machine gun causing many casualties, Private Robertson dashed to an opening on the flank, rushed the machine gun and, after a desperate struggle with the crew, killed four and then turned the gun on the remainder who, overcome by the fierceness of his onslaught, were running towards their own lines. His gallant work enabled the platoon to advance. He inflicted many more casualties among the enemy and then, carrying the machine gun, he led his platoon to the final position, and got the gun into action, firing on the retreating enemy, who by this time were quite demoralised by the fire brought to bear on them. During the consolidation, Private Robertson's most determined use of the machine gun kept down the fire of the enemy's snipers. His courage and his coolness cheered his comrades and inspired them to the finest efforts. Later, when two of our snipers were badly wounded in front of our trench, he went out and carried one of them in under very severe fire. He was killed just as he returned with the second man'

He is the only one of the Canadian VCs killed at Passchendaele who has a known grave; he lies in Tyne Cot. He appears to have been quite

View to Passchendaele Church from Crest Farm Canadian Memorial. It was near this road (which did not exist in 1917) that Robertson won his VC.

a character of an enormous Highland family – six sisters and four brothers. He himself seems to have been larger than life, enormous man as he was. His fame spread amongst the locomotive engineers, his peacetime occupation. A Canadian paper reported that at 'a great gathering of locomotive engineers in Cleveland [USA] after Private Robertson's gallant deed and his fate became known, that gathering of 77,000 strong men from Canada and the United States rose and a standing vote honoured the memory of the first Locomotive Engineer VC'. His widowed mother received the VC in Medicine Hat, where the Lieutenant-Governor commented, 'This cross is only a small thing, its cost is very little, but it has engraved on it the words: "For Valour" which mean a great deal. Money can do much – with money titles can be bought, but money cannot buy the Victoria Cross.'

The Germans attempted to recapture the village later in the day, but Passchendaele had finally fallen. On the left things had gone well on the right of the 1st Divisional attack; Mosselmarkt fell much more easily than might have been anticipated, and in particular the principal pill-box fell with few losses, despite disgorging four officers and fifty men as prisoners. The real problems were away over to the left, where the 3rd (Toronto) Battalion faced considerable difficulties and where the last of Canada's nine Victoria Crosses in the Passchendaele campaign was won.

The 1st and 2nd Battalions had the advantage of attacking either side of the Gravenstafel-Mosselmarkt road; the 3rd was separated from them by very swampy ground and had purely artillery support on its left. The 3rd Battalions objective was Goudberg, but it faced another one of the large, formidable German pill-boxes that were such a feature of this campaign - this one at Vine Cottage. The attack against this particular obstacle came from the higher ground on the north west, with the intention of taking it and then pushing back northwards. The pill-box was entirely constructed within the old farm building. The attack was launched upon it from three sides, but the heavy ground and the defensive fire made the grenades ineffectual; morale was not helped by the cries of the wounded, who were left, perforce, exposed under the driving rain, the cold winds and open to German fire and artillery shells.

It was at this point that the thirty-two year old Corporal Barron, brought up in the Highlands, took a decisive interest in affairs. *Thirty Canadian VCs* takes up the story,

'Our men started to attack once more and, as they rose to their feet, a diversion occurred to the front. Corporal Barron, a

**C F Barron
VC**

Lewis gunner, had worked his way round to the flank with his weapon, and was knocking out the German crews, one after the other, with his well directed fire. Completely exposed, he directed his gun unconcerned by the point blank shooting of the enemy until he had silenced two of the opposing batteries [sic]. Then without waiting for his comrades, he charged the remaining position with the bayonet, getting in among the gunners and killing four of them before the rest of the platoon could arrive. The slackening of the heavy fire gave the Canadians the chance to get well forward and in a moment they were about the position. The guns Barron had been unable to reach kept up a heavy fire until our fellows were on top of them, when most of the crews surrendered, while others attempted to escape to the rear. But the Canadians had lost too many of their comrades to feel merciful, and they were infuriated at the general morale of men who would maintain murderous shooting until imminent danger pressed and then calmly sue for mercy. They took few prisoners. Corporal Barron had not finished his good work. Turning the enemy's guns about, he opened fire upon the retreating Germans, catching the groups upon the hillside, and shooting them down with such good effect that hardly a man escaped.'

Rear of a pill-box with a German gun partially buried after a British bombardment.

This quite successful day cost the Canadians 734 dead and some 1500 other casualties.

The end of Third Ypres: the attack of 10 November 1917

The final action in the Third Battle of Ypres, which had begun some three-and-a-half months earlier on 31 July, and with such great possibilities, was to come to an end here, about five miles north east of Ypres

The objectives, as described above, were very limited – this final phase of the battle only involved three [1st, 1st (Canadian) and 2nd (Canadian)] divisions on a very narrow front, which enabled the Germans to concentrate their artillery upon them, especially after the attack was over. The left of the attack (ie the British part) had gone well as the advance began at 6.45 am, but disaster struck when 1/South Wales Borderers veered too far off to the right. When the inevitable German counter-attack went in soon after 7 am, it found this gap and was able completely to cut off the bulk of the left battalion, 2/Royal Munster Fusiliers, which consequently suffered horrendous losses - 13 officers and 400 other ranks. The Borderers, left with their flank in the air, were forced to withdraw to their start line. The neighbouring Canadian Brigade was more successful, capturing Venture Farm and several field pieces; the debacle on its left meant that it had to throw out a protective left flank and meant that the British were creating a dangerously small salient in the German line.

The right of the attack was to be by the 20th (Central Ontario) Battalion on its own; its task was to advance the line about five hundred yards, taking the line northerly along the ridge. The men were brought up to Hamburg Farm, where the planked track came to an end, from there to Hillside Farm and beyond was the pill-box that was battalion headquarters. There had been a potentially disastrous start to the journey.

'As the Battalion detrained at the Ypres siding three great German Gotha planes, escorted by a dozen smaller and faster aircraft, sailed over Ypres, circled and came right overhead. A deluge of small bombs was expected at any moment, but the planes sailed off to the south-eastward, probably not having seen the expectant battalion. This was the first time the large Gothas had been seen, and it was difficult not to look up and gaze at them as they glistened overhead in the bright sunlight. After the first glance there was not a move in the battalion, which was in the act of assembling for the march to Potijze, and it is probably

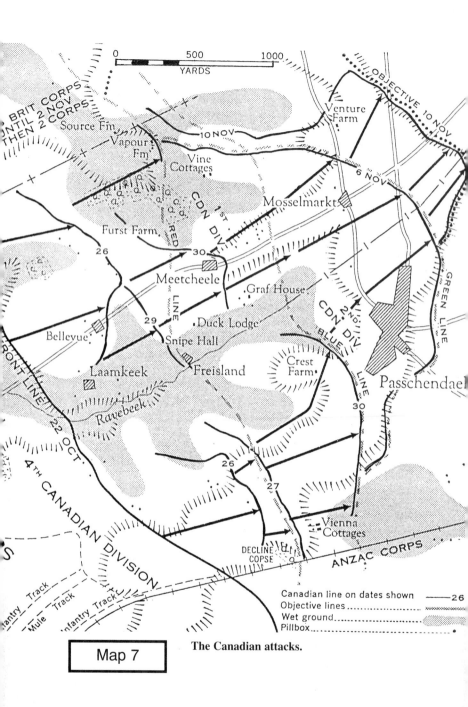

The Canadian attacks.

Canadian line on dates shown ——26
Objective lines ....
Wet ground...........................
Pillbox....................................

Map 7

90

due to the discipline of each one present that the unit avoided casualties.'[2]

This problem with German bombers is frequently mentioned in unit accounts of Passchendaele, as well as in numbers of individual accounts. This campaign witnessed the first major battle where bombers are mentioned with such regularity; no later significant battle would take place without their menace being felt or feared by the troops on the ground.

The battalion headquarters was in a former German pill-box, as had been many of the unit and advanced formation headquarters during this latter phase of Third Ypres. This one was typical of the larger variety:

'a solid structure of reinforced concrete about twenty four feet by twenty two feet outside with walls three feet thick; the concrete roof was reinforced by steel rails and would turn any but the heaviest shells. The one entrance faced the enemy, but was closed to their direct fire by a heavy mass of solid concrete built inside the walls and forming two passageways, one to the right and one to the left, both leading to the structure's one room. That room was about sixteen feet by ten feet and eight feet to the roof; machine gun slits, facing our lines, and a small hole in the roof provided the only ventilation, for a blanket hung at all times in the entrance; the only light was from the well-known candles. In that confined headquarters were crowded the headquarters of the 18th and 20th battalion for the next three days. The Germans, knowing that no other convenient shelter existed for use as a headquarter, shelled it almost without pause. Bodies that could not be buried in such an inferno lay all around it, and would have to lie until the operations ceased.'

A group of wounded Canadians, with a German prisoner, alongside a shattered pill-box.

German casualties during the battle for Passchendaele.

The advance was rapid and without great difficulty; however a similar problem to that which had faced the 1st (Imperial) Division threatened when it was discovered that the neighbouring 7th Battalion on the left had overshot their objective and veered too far to the north; this gap was filled by some platoons of the 20th, and the line was ultimately

The final yards covered, the village on the ridge that had cost so many lives, was finally captured. View from near Crest Farm.

brought back to its original objective because of creating an even more unmanageable salient into the German lines. The situation was bad enough, as the Germans were able to turn the batteries of several German corps upon the new line, leading an Australian to comment in his diary that the attack was, 'on a very narrow front – almost as bad as at Pozières; and the Germans... concentrated an enormous amount of artillery on to the area which we took, and the British were driven in... The night is simply vile and the day too... If the Canadians can hold on they are wonderful troops'.³ The 20th also faced a couple of determined counter-attacks, but these were broken up by the artillery or by the battalion's own firepower. To make themselves less vulnerable, the battalion had been pushed forward and positioned in small trenches and shell holes well over to the eastern side of the ridge.

11 November dawned sunny, for once in the while. A report came back that Sergeant C Stevens had gone five hundred yards into No Man's Land and had returned with important documents. Actually, this soldier had not been inspired by military diligence but was engaged in that age old practice of finding souvenirs on the battlefield.

'Emerging into No Man's Land, he extended the sphere of exploration by going a good deal further than his predecessors [ie those who had also been on the lookout for desirable objects] *and came upon two men lying face down in the mud. Rifles, with bayonets fixed, lay beside them. From the first he removed a pocket-book, found nothing else, and stooped over the body to get a flashlight lying beside the second. The "corpse" chose that moment to talk in its sleep... A few minutes later a badly alarmed sergeant arrived in our lines out of breath and clutching a pocket-book containing the "valuable documents" mentioned in the report.'*

Passchendaele Church once more looms large in the January gloom – resurrected from the destruction of war.

Road to Broodseinde
and Zonnebeke

This aerial photograph was taken 27 October 1917 and clearly shows the
devastation caused to the village of Passchendaele by British artillery.

Present day village of Passchendaele, looking north west, showing the distinctive curved road around the church and the village square.

The ordeal of the battalion came to an end with its relief that night – but it took almost ten hours to complete.

'After trailing through the mire, the Battalion assembled there [Seine Dump] in due course. The struggle to get out alive had been so great that many of the walking wounded died from exhaustion. All were almost unrecognisable. Everyone had three-day-old beards. Faces, hands and clothing were covered with mud. A few had no shoes, several had no puttees, many had no helmets, but none cared much. A special party from rear headquarters was at Seine Dump to carry the Lewis guns, arms and equipment so that the men could walk the rest of the way without encumbrance – a happy thought on someone's part. After breakfast and a brief rest the march back to the tents at Potijze was begun...'

This could describe the experience of all the battalions that had fought in the battle for the village – British, Canadian, New Zealand or German. Whatever, the village was never to feature so prominently again in British military history. Passchendaele fell rapidly to the Germans in their Lys offensive, launched in April 1918, bringing bitter recriminations from many Canadians at the wasteful loss of life for a position that was lost within minutes. The Canadians had 15,654 casualties for their month or so on the Passchendaele front. The Germans pushed the Ypres Salient to its narrowest limits around that town since the war had begun; but Ypres did not fall, and the offensive failed. Passchendaele did not see British arms again, for it was an Army under the command of Albert, King of the Belgians, and Belgian troops, that finally liberated the red brick stained mud that had been Passchendaele in September 1918.

1 *Canadian Expeditionary Force 1914 - 1919*,
    Colonel GWL Nicholson CD
2 *History of the 20th Canadian Battalion in the Great War 1914 - 1919*,
    Major DJ Corrigall DSO MC
3 *The AIF in France* Vol IV, CEW Bean

With the Germans pushed back beyond the village it is much safer for these men to stand up in groups and to walk around, as these Australian troops are doing.

Chapter Six

PASSCHENDAELE: THE GERMAN EXPERIENCE

For this part of the book I am enormously grateful for the hard work of Ralph Whitehead, a friend of mine in the United States, who has spent considerable hours translating parts of German histories for me. This is devotion above and beyond the call of duty, as those who have seen some of these German formation and unit histories will testify - Gothic script takes a considerable training to master.

Nearly all of the writing on Passchendaele concentrates on the British and Dominion experience; that of the Germans is skated over. This gives rise to an apparent feeling held in popular circles in Great Britain that her armies almost uniquely suffered the miserable - indeed hideous - conditions of the final weeks of the Third Ypres. They also work on the supposition that the British senior commanders were also uniquely awful. This chapter aims to show something of what the German soldier endured, and includes some very trenchant criticism of the actions of some of their generals.

The Passchendaele battle involved the use of no less than eighty-six German divisions, twenty two of them being pushed into the battle more than once. This compares to the fifty-one that Britain and her Dominions employed – though it must be taken into account that the German divisions were approximately a third smaller in numbers of bayonets than the British, i.e. they had three fewer infantry battalions; even then, the British total approximates to about seventy German divisions. It does mean, however, that the vast majority of the British army on the Western Front experienced the horrors of the Passchendaele battle - more so by some seven divisions than those who suffered in the longer (by about five weeks) and bloodier (by about 190,000 casualties) Somme offensive.

The 92nd Infantry Regiment
(For this section refer to New Zealand's Contribution 4 - 12 October 1917)

This section takes extracts from the 92nd Regimental History, a part of the 20th Division which had its recruiting origins from Hanover. This Division had extensive experience on both the Eastern and Western Front; immediately before being thrown into the Flanders battle the Division had been on the Russian Front (for the third time);

Belgian postcard printed in Flemish and sent by a German soldier to his '*Lovely little cheeky monkey*'. This town was a staging post for troops headed to the front.

no sooner had it arrived at Roulers on 27 September after an eight day trans-Europe rail crossing from Riga, in Latvia, than it was thrown into the Flanders battle north of Zonnebeke.

The Division consisted of three regiments, the 77th, 79th, and 92nd, each of which roughly equated to a British brigade, except that from the spring of 1915 the Germans steadily reduced their regiments to three battalions instead of four, a process which the British undertook in 1918. German battalions at the time described in this book had bayonet strengths of about 800. There were four companies in each battalion, but they were numbered throughout the regiment from 1 to 12. The 92nd Regiment's battalions were designated Leib (Body), I and II. The theory was that a regiment was commanded by a Colonel (Oberst) with a Lieutenant-Colonel as second in command, a battalion by a Major and a company by a Captain. In practice a regiment was usually being commanded by a Major, a battalion by a Captain and a company by a Lieutenant. NCOs carried out many of the functions of British junior officers; an *Unteroffizier*, whom many people think was an officer cadet, was not an officer, but rather a corporal.[1]

The Regiment served on the Flanders battlefield for about a week; it was withdrawn from the line on 10 October and by the 14th it was in Cambrai, and served on the Queant sector until February 1918.

The history starts its account of its time in the area of Passchendaele bleakly. 'The 4th of October arrived. The blackest day in the history of the regiment, indeed it weaved around to form a halo that no one could take from it.' The cataclysm that followed was ascribed to the

The ruins of Zonnebeke Church from the rear with German dugout.

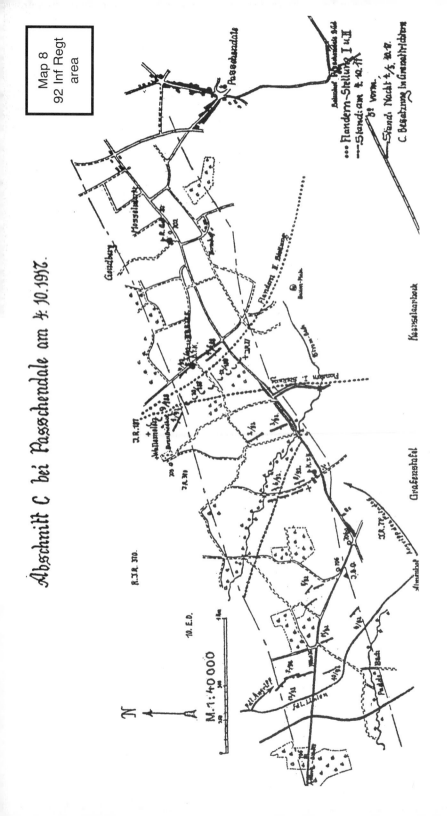

Abschnitt C bei Passchendale am 4.10.1917.

Map 8
92 Inf Regt
area

German signallers operating from a Regimental HQ overlooking the Salient.

uncertain weather, which favoured British preparation and the fortune of luck; in addition the regiment had had no time to adapt to its new circumstances.

The 4th Guard Infantry Division was preparing for a counter-attack to try and regain lost ground around Zonnebeke. They were all ready to launch their attack when the British barrage fell upon them.

'The attack of the Guards Division was knocked to pieces at the start. Twelve English divisions stood behind this unheard of fire wall, about 100,000 men, arm in arm, ready to attack. A great battle day of unheard of proportions then rose up on Flanders fields. The iron birds sounded with the wildest singing and struck with frightful agitation. The splinters whistled through the air, whistling and roaring. Craters disappeared, then rose anew. The Leib Battalion was situated in the wildest insane whirlpool. The results of the bombardment quickly struck into it. The bodies were riddled, the pulses racing. Time crawled by. Seconds seemed like hours. The uncertainty was frightful. The throats of the fighters tightened with nameless dread. Who could deny this? Their eyes were veiled. Did you become concerned? Were you going to die without the enemy appearing one more time? Many situated there became dull and felt no more; that they were finished, expecting to become smashed in the monstrous chaos each moment. Many prayed; perhaps for some it was a long time since they had last

richtergelände vor Paschendaele mit Blick auf Ypern 3. Oktober 1917.   *W.*

Sketches made by a German artist at the time of the battle: *'Cratered ground at Passchendaele looking towards Ypres'.* **Below:** *Bombardment near Passchedaele.*

prayed. 'My God, spare me'. And in their prayer they mixed a small glimmer of hope – they clung to the fact that they were still alive with passion. Others held out firmly on trust. The will to live united them with the readiness to die. 'Lord, thy will be done'.

The vivid account goes on,

> *'they hope, to sell their lives as dearly as possible. This weakness is frightful. Their face is distorted in grim rage. The fist firmly holds the rifle. All too often the weapons are choked up and become useless. Each repairs them with feverish haste. The eyes attempted to see through the haze, the ears strained to listen, banishing the danger by the sudden appearance of the enemy in front of them. The enemy's batteries drummed further. All of the minenwerfers* [trench mortars] *were buried and the machine guns, for the greater part, suffered a similar fate. A soldier, according to the extent of his wounds, was placed to the side or rolled into the craters. Life was slowly, sluggishly fleeing out of the wounds. No wild pain. They felt the fullest fulfilment of their life as they died, which from the beginning had been death in battle. With parched lips and burning sight the living still waited, crouched between the dead and wounded. All telephone and telegraph positions were destroyed in the shortest space of time. Smoke covered the position. A smoke screen rolled incessantly over the battlefield and hindered everybody's sight.'*

The New Zealand attack commenced (note that the German clock was one hour ahead of British time – some things never change!).

> *'About 8 am the glowing fire wall sprang with a start and reached out at fifty metre leaps towards the rear falling in front*

Am 4. Oklb. 17. morg. 6 Uhr. Regts. Gef. Stand bei Paschendaele. engl. Trommelfeuer. · W. L.

Trench mortar and projectile. Mortars such as this were particularly feared by the Allied soldiers because of their accuracy and their destructive power.

of and behind the 5th and 11th companies, which suffered relatively few casualties. About this time the smoke dispersed.'

The front battalion (the Leib Battalion) found no enemy in front of them, but the division on their right (10th Ersatz) was being pushed backwards as the British followed on closely behind a very sharp and short assault barrage. Hill 32 (to the immediate west and south of Boetleer) had to be held 'unconditionally' as it 'was the key point of the regiment'. Meanwhile the 4th Guards Division was being forced back and the British barrage had caused havoc with their support troops. The 79th and 77th regiments (on the 92nd's left) were pushed back with them.

'Meanwhile a wounded man from the 370th Regiment (on the right) reported to the regimental staff of the 92nd that the enemy had broken through his regiment. At 8.30 am a messenger dog reached I Battalion with a report from the Leib Battalion that the Englishmen (sic) *had also broken through there.'*

This battalion found its right flank in the air as its neighbours withdrew. The 2nd and 3rd companies were ordered forward to reinforce the 6th and the 8th, situated on the further side of the

German soldiers partialy buried after a bombardment.

Stroombeek/Ravebeek (nomenclature of the streams gets complicated; the position referred to here is north of the Gravenstafel - Mosselmarkt road, a few hundred yards to the west of Peter Pan). The 1st and 4th companies were ordered forward from their support positions north of the Bellevue crossroads. They

'found themselves in an advance through swamp and craters towards a barrier of a size never seen before; on the other side of the bank of the Stroombeek an orgy of fire, colour and light fell on them. Was it possible to traverse these blazing, smoking fires? Their hearts were wildly beating and threatened to burst. High explosives and smoke shells mixed with the shrapnel followed so quickly after each other that all was covered in a dense haze. Casualties stumbled to the rear. Craters arose, sucking the warrior into its depths. Several were hurled into them and disappeared. Gefreiter (Lance Corporal) *Stuhlmuller, 1st*

Company, leader of a light machine gun section, had his weapon shot into small pieces. The men came forward slowly, individually. The connection between and within the companies was totally lost ...a large number of soldiers asked themselves whether they should stay in the fire in the remnants of the destroyed Flanders I position or withdraw. Some made their way into the sector of the 77th Regiment (on the left) or were dispersed. Only the bravest, first of all Lieutenants Lemmermann and Knoche, 1st Company, and Lieutenant Hemmpel, 4th Company, hurled themselves into this fire. Both orderlies of the last officer, Gefreiter Stubig and Musketier Jünemann, were torn to pieces next to him by a direct hit. He finally reached the 2nd Company position with nine men. ...Lieutenant Bähr, commander of the 3rd Company, had prepared a report for regimental headquarters sent before their arrival that the

The Germans did not escape the appalling conditions at Passchendaele. Here a partially flooded trench is being endured by these German infantrymen.

A view from the German trenches on the high ground above Ypres.

position of his company still held. It was his last report. Towards 10 am he had already found his death, whilst his first report of his disposition reached the regiment at 1.30 pm. With his death went a distinguished leader, always in the toughest spot. Honour these men!'

Disaster had struck the Leib and II Battalion.

'The death of Flanders was thrown with a bitter cry from the breast of the warrior... the terror, which so many had marked out in their fantasies, would be fulfilled here. Here a hand grenade cracked, there a flashing bayonet. Here a last cry, there a quiet sigh. The Flanders ground greedily soaked up the blood ... the last glance that came with the fatal wound was the dug up and shattered earth which ground down their shattered bodies. Their souls walked up the road to Valhalla.'

The history goes on to record the bravery and heroism of numerous individuals, 'the machine gun misfired and the only Unteroffizier who was able to operate it sank down, badly wounded'. Men surrendered, hopelessly outnumbered; now the attack moved on to the combined 10th and 12th companies, situated forward of Bellevue. They even tried a counter-attack, which led to the death of Lieutenant Kerber,

'with him went a soldier, who through his cheerful sunny nature had understood when the men were in a momentary depressed move and he always caused confidence to flow into

106

*them again. He often stood the test in battle, he brought to his
brow the bloody laurel of the hero. Honour his memory!'*

By 9.15 am (German time) the staffs of both the Leib and II Battalions
had been killed or captured and the 6th and 8th companies had been
reduced to forty effectives. Heavy fighting took place around Waterloo
(marked KIK on the German map). A machine gun had kept up a
sustained fire on the advancing New Zealanders.

> *'Now the enemy appeared and threw hand grenades through
> the slits which destroyed the machine gun; through them the
> enemy opened fire with pistols and rifles. The dug out was tightly
> filled with the wounded and the shots produced new wounded
> everywhere. A monstrous disorder now followed in the smoke-
> enveloped bunker. Everyone pressed towards the exit, but
> Medical Officer Dr Bartsch did not allow them to exit without
> first having a Red Cross flag in the hand. A pistol shot stretched
> him out.'*

The history records others who went out and were shot – although it
does admit that the bunker was also an ammunition dump.

> *'No New Zealanders ventured into the bunker. When the fury*

**This German was wounded, treated and bandaged, and then blown up
and killed before he could be moved out of the firing line to safety.**

of the attackers had subsided they allowed the remainder to come out of the dugout. Given the situation, there was no further talk of resistance. Hauptmann (Captain) *Kobus, who they had found on the other side of the bunker, left with a pocket book to wave and offered the capitulation.'*

Elsewhere the 6th and 8th companies had surrendered.

'Undoubtedly out of rage over the heavy casualties of the New Zealanders, they shot the unarmed Lieutenant Leonhard, whose name has so often brought forth honour, with their machine gun. Also individual soldiers would be mercilessly shot down. The prisoners would be fully plundered. Even the buttons would be cut away from them; afterwards they were sewn up together as souvenirs. The manner in which they did this was only a little different from the coloured troops of the French. Under the protection of a large Red Cross flag the enemy assembled the prisoners and directed them to the rear. The companies of I Battalion from the other bank of the Strombeek and the 5th and 11th companies were impotent as the men were led away.'

These last named two companies were the unwitting authors of their own fate. Up to now they had managed to remain undetected, on seeing two German aircraft overhead they tried to signal their position by placing signal cloths so that assistance could be got to them. It was to no avail, but instead revealed their position to the British artillery and heavy machine guns. Their position was overrun.

'The New Zealanders, who were under the influence of alcohol [a common story about attacking troops and almost certainly not true], *plundered everything from the prisoners. What the enemy did not take in the forward line in their haste was later taken away from the troops when they were transported into captivity.'*

The 20th Division continued to hold the Bellevue Ridge, despite the weakness of both its flanks; it received reinforcements in the course of the day, and in the end the line was stabilised.

'The terrain gained by the enemy amounted to 1 – 1$^{1}/_{2}$ kilometres and it cost him the heaviest of casualties. The artillery barrage and machine-gun fire had together often shot up entire columns. The Englishmen had not attained their objectives, "It is a long way to Tipperary, it is a long way to Passchendaele" the English Tommy swore. However the flower of the 20th Division covered the earth of Flanders. General Ludendorff, in the army report of the day, correctly said, "The heroism of the German

troops in Flanders could not be surpassed by anything".'

The history notes that the British allowed the Germans to collect their casualties the next day unmolested (a courtesy repaid by the Germans after the battle of 12 October); the men were relieved on the night of the 7th. All the regiments rearranged their three battalions into two weak companies instead of the usual four. Some of the Division had already left the sector when a new attack was launched on the 9th. Units of the 77th Regiment and 79th Regiment (the latter had suffered least in the battle of the 4th) were already marching out of the sector when the Division was recalled shortly after 8 am.

'The order: "Turn! March!" hit like a bolt of lightning. One could still hardly grasp it that one would escape this murder. The bodies were emaciated, the nerves were stretched to their limit. Now the cruel game begins again. Many a curse escaped past the teeth.'

The regiment had a big butcher's bill for its ten days in Flanders: 24 officers, and 1,185 other ranks, of whom 10 officers were killed and 385 other ranks were known to be dead, although a large number of the 580 missing were likely to be so as well. These bodies 'were never found. Many were covered up and buried unmarked, others were swallowed up in the craters filled with water and mud'. The history comments that the survivors were, 'profoundly shaken mentally'. The Divisional commander told his men that, 'the thrust into the heart of our Fatherland has been victoriously repulsed. The sacrifices which this division had to experience has also brought success'.

The flowery language in which this history is written is something one would never find in a British regimental history; but it is not untypical of the manner in which these histories were written in the German and indeed other continental armies. *Storm of Steel* and *Copse*

A shell bursting near a stretcher party east of the Menin Road.

Captured German troops assist with British wounded, acting as stretcher-bearers behind the lines.

125 are both easily accessible memoirs in English of a German soldier, Ernst Jünger; both these books have been recently reprinted (1996).

A more general German history is rather less 'purple' in its language, but still sounds alien to English ears. It describes the situation on the night of 23 October,

> '...the drizzle became a steady rain. The troops suffered horribly. Warm food could be brought up virtually nowhere. The removal of the considerable quantity of wounded was only done extremely slowly. The rain fell also without end the next morning Under such conditions an English attack was out of the question. With wet feet, freezing, no dry clothes, staring and motionless lay friend and foe in opposite craters. Compelled by idleness the Englishmen fired some thousands of shells of heavy calibre to plummet down on the debris of Passchendaele. The last remnants of the walls were thrown over. A couple of pill-boxes built into the cellars collapsed and buried their occupants. The tremendous thunder hits of the explosions blotted out all other sounds at the front. A cloud of grey fog clung to the shallow ridge and slowly crept downward into the boggy country. When we trod upon the house ruins we did not recognise one single stone. Passchendaele was no longer.'

It describes the fighting of 30 October as 'gruesome and bitter'. It seems to think that the Canadian objectives were far more ambitious than in fact they were. November arrived, and with it frost and

110

weariness: 'the divisions are no longer what they had been earlier, not as defenders and not as attackers'. It notes that battles could be won by 'the actions of small numbers of troops or that four machine guns could turn back the ruthless force of an attack wave of an entire division', a situation hitherto 'inconceivable'.

The loss of Passchendaele on 6 November is noted in a terse sentence: 'By the afternoon Passchendaele is lost'. It also noted exceptionally heavy losses among the defending regiments of the 4th and 11th divisions. The decision was taken to launch counter-attacks to try and regain the site of the village.

'Wasted time begins back and forth between the command positions. The Group (Ypres) urges them to make the most extreme speed, the division (11th) warned them to make prudent preparations, because when one has a strong adversary they necessarily want to retain their gains.

'The battalions sat under the heaviest fire and had considerable losses. When the formations were finally organised for their objectives in the counter-attack they ended up in the dark and they were scattered. The Group had a contrary opinion, they considered dusk to be the most favourable opportunity to attain their objectives.

'Under the embracing wreath of the battle the village was as before with its noise, its biting colours and its iron splinters. Several attempts by the Canadians to advance towards the east were repulsed. They remained in the pincers. Everyone waits for the arrival of the experienced counter-attack troops.

'But the Group urges the immediate execution of the attack. The main strength of the thrust is placed on the area north of the village. From here it would turn to the south and cut it off.'

Delays follow – Bavarian troops on the right were switched to the command of the 11th Division; but first they had to acclimatise themselves to the new situation. 'Precious time is lost over and over.' It grew dark and the waiting battalions were still suffering considerable casualties.

'Finally at 7 pm the fully manned support line reports. The attack order is given. However the artillery preparation is not satisfactory. It has already used up part of the ammunition that was specifically for the counter-attack by midday, because the order about the postponement of the attack did not reach them until very late. Many batteries did not know that the attack was not arranged for the evening.

Passchendaele village prior to the onslaught.

'The span of time between the issuing of attack orders and its launch is too short; many battalions still have not received the order at all, while their neighbours have already left their craters to go forward. The night and the rain increases the chaos. The English box barrage fires with undiminished force... Finally at 11 pm the Group officially lifts the attack order; it had happened effectively a lot earlier.

'Total chaos amongst the fighting troops was the consequence of this back and forth movement; their organisation took place in the course of the night under the hardest conditions and with considerable losses. Passchendaele remains in the hands of the Canadians.'

After the attacks of 10 November the history reports simply: 'The Battle is finished'. It continues,

'Not long after the first snow falls from the grey heavens into the water filled craters. At first it mixes with the mud and blends with the mushy mass. However one morning it remains and covers the place of horror with its white blanket... This strip of land gradually falls asleep.'

1 *History of the German Army which participated in the war (1914 - 1918).* LSE 1989;

2 *German Army Handbook April 1918*, Arms and Armour Press 1977.

The destruction of Passchendaele village is under way – preliminary
shelling takes its toll on the houses.

This huge, multi-purpose German bunker is in a field near St Julien, one of the few remaining from the war. It gives a good indication of the formidable strength of the defences that had to be overcome.

Touring the Battlefield

Walks and Car Tour

Dochy Farm West
Dochy Farm - the New Zealand Advance
The Canadian Attack - North
The Canadian Attack - South
A Car Tour - the Northern Part of the Battlefield

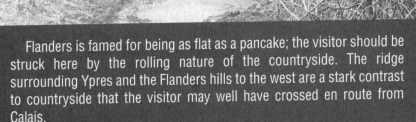

Flanders is famed for being as flat as a pancake; the visitor should be struck here by the rolling nature of the countryside. The ridge surrounding Ypres and the Flanders hills to the west are a stark contrast to countryside that the visitor may well have crossed en route from Calais.

Detailed maps are very difficult to come by in Belgium. The 1:50000 maps that are relevant are 28 and 19-20; inevitably the battlefield does not fit on the one map! The Ieper (28) map is obtainable at the Tourist Office in Ypres. The 1:25000 series are obtainable, it seems to me, only in Brussels or by ordering them from a good map shop in the UK. The relevant ones are 28/3-4 Geluveld - Moorsele and 20/7-8 Staden - Roeselare which covers the relatively small part of the area covered in this book to the north and north west of Passchendaele.

Walk 1. Dochy Farm West

[This walk may be done in a car.]

This walk begins at **Dochy Farm New British Cemetery**. The farm itself was on the other side of the road about fifty yards into the fields to the west **[1]**, more or less in line with Tyne Cot. On 4 October the cemetery was in No Man's Land and the farm was a part of the German Front Line. Looking from the west side of the road there are excellent views across almost all of the battlefield discussed in this book, from Gravenstafel on the half left and the Bellevue Spur leading up to the notable tower to the north of Passchendaele, then to the west, in front of you, the valley of the Hannebeek with Abraham Heights and Passchendaele beyond and then half right the massive cemetery at Tyne Cot. To the south east the road runs in to Zonnebeke.

After coming out of the cemetery **turn right** along the road to Zonnebeke, and **almost immediately turn right** along a minor road. The ground falls away sharply to the left as you go along, and in the middle distance may be seen the brick factory at Zonnebeke with its distinctive range of chimneys. *Bremen redoubt* **[3]** and its enormous German-built bunker is on this side of the factory buildings at the edge of the big clay pit – it was in excavations for clay that the bunker was discovered in the early 80s. The second track down to the left lies on *Hill 37* **[5]**, which marks the line achieved by the British on 20 September. The buildings near this track were known as *Cabbage Cottages*.

This walk helps to emphasise the surprisingly undulating nature of the area – there is a lot of dead ground and one can begin to understand the logic behind the succession of German defence lines.

Where the road bears away to the left there is a track going straight on. At this junction there is a farm which stands almost on the site of *Gallipoli* **[4]**, an advanced battalion headquarters for the New Zealanders on the edge of *Hill 35*. Natural cover was – and is still – scarce in the area, and so reinforced cellars were used by both sides. The farms were frequently used by brigades and battalions as headquarters, as dumps and as aid posts; not only because use could be made of their cellars, which more often than not the Germans had reinforced for their own purposes, but there was also reasonable quality hard standing, however heavy the shelling – and anything was better than the boggy morass to which the fields were reduced. After the war many of the farms were rebuilt on the same location, or very close to it.

As the ground drops away, at another sharp bend in the road, on the left hand side is *Pommern Castle* **[6]**. This was used progressively by battalions and brigades as headquarters as the front worked its way eastwards, It was to here that the sorely

BERLIN WOOD

ABRAHAM HEIGHTS

A captured pill-box in front of Passchendaele in use as a Forward Aid Post.

tried men from the PPCLI came in the early hours of 1 November after their successful onslaught on the Bellevue Spur; from here the infantry track would enable them to get back to the relative safety of the rear areas. It was to here that the Brigade commander came to congratulate them. Pommern Castle stood on the limit of the British advance on 31 July 1917.

Continue to the cross roads, which more or less follows that line, and **turn left**; just beyond the next road junction on the right is *Spree Farm* **[7]**. For the New Zealand attacks this was a major medical station, men would receive emergency treatment and then be sent on down the road to Wieltje where there was an Advanced Dressing Station and where wheeled transport could get casualties away. Between the two points was *Bridge House* **[9]**, reached further along the road, which was used as the base for stretcher bearers to relieve each other.

Bridge House stands on the old German second line, and fell to the attack on 31 July; although the New Zealanders did not make use of the protection of this farm as a dressing station it was used as such in the attack on Polygon Wood at the end of September.

Three or four hundred yards further down the road towards Wieltje is the site of the dugout where Captain Noel Chavasse VC* had his aid post and near which he received the wounds on 2 August 1917 which were to prove mortal. He was the only

PASSCHENDAELE CHURCH SPIRE

HAALEN COPSE

TYNE COT CEMETERY

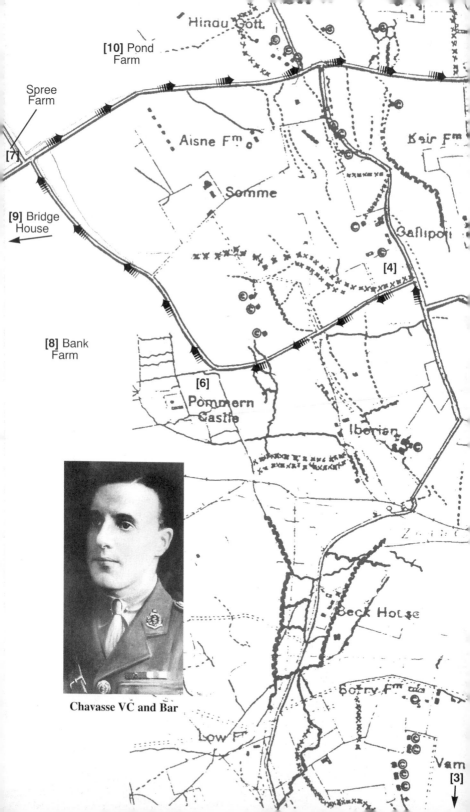

[10] Pond Farm

Spree Farm

[7]

[9] Bridge House

Hingu Gott.

Aisne F^m

Somme

Keir F^m

Gallipoli

[4]

[8] Bank Farm

[6]

Pommern Castle

Iberian

Beck House

Chavasse VC and Bar

Sorry F^m

Low F^m

Vam

[3]

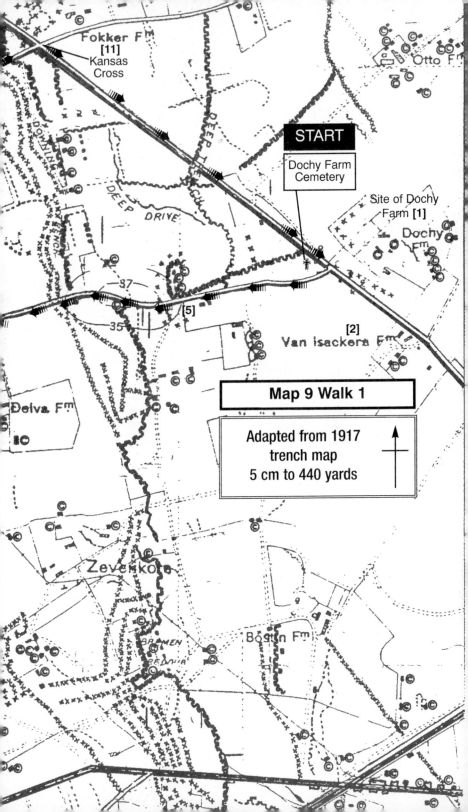

Fokker Fᵐ
[11]
Kansas
Cross

START

Dochy Farm
Cemetery

DEEP

DEEP DRIVE

Site of Dochy
Farm [1]

Dochy
Fᵐ

Otto Fᵐ

DOWNING

37

[5]

35

[2]

Van Isackers Fᵐ

Map 9 Walk 1

Delva Fm

Adapted from 1917
trench map
5 cm to 440 yards

Zevenkote

Bremen

Boston Fm

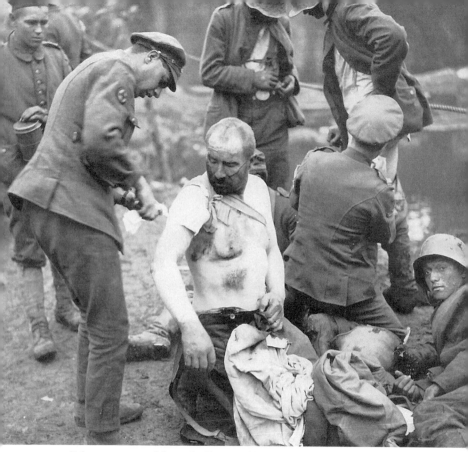

Prisoners captured from the German 20th Division being treated at a New Zealand Division Advance Dressing Station near Wieltje 5 October 1917. The preceding day had been dubbed 'a black day' by the Germans.

person to win two Victoria Crosses in the Great War and only the second person to achieve this distinction.

Retrace your steps and follow the road to Kansas Cross. The second farm to your left after passing Spree Farm, situated a hundred yards or so off the road, is *Pond Farm* **[10]**. Close to the outbuildings on the western side is a fine pill-box. Currie (see page 49), then a brigade commander, had his headquarters here during the Second Battle of Ypres in late April 1915.

Continue towards *Kansas Cross* **[11]**, bearing in mind that all around here artillery pieces of all calibres were stranded or being manhandled into position at various stages of the Passchendaele campaign. It must have been a quite extraordinary sight especially when the sounds of death and cries of the wounded, whinnying horses, shells, the smells of gas, cordite and blood were combined with hordes of men scurrying around, the flashes and concussions of shells – a Dante's inferno, most terrifying at night.

At Kansas Cross **turn right** and return to your car. The German line before the 4 October attack was in the fields fifty to a hundred yards or so on your left, more or less following the line of the road.

Walk 2. Dochy Farm – the New Zealand Advance

This walk can be slightly amended to be done by car

Park the car at Dochy Farm New British Cemetery and walk **south eastwards** along the road **to Zonnebeke**. The farm on your right is Van Isackere (sometimes known as Van Isackers) Farm **[1]** which was where the 44th Battalion CEF waited before moving up to the line on 26 October. On the other side of the road, almost directly north, and a hundred yards or so into the fields, is the site of Dochy Farm, which had been a significant feature in the German defences. You are now walking out of the New Zealand Division sector and into that of 3rd Australian Division for the attack on 4 October.

After another hundred yards or so **turn left** along a narrow metalled road. This gently climbs up the ridge, and an excellent view of Tyne Cot is to be had. In due course Springfield **[2]** will be passed, which was a German strongpoint. Off to the left, in the valley of the Hannebeek/Nieuwebeek, may be seen Bordeaux Farm **[3]** and Boethoek **[4]**; Boethoek was to serve as a Battalion headquarters both for New Zealanders and Canadians as the battle progressed.

At the **T Junction** a farm, Beecham **[5]**, will be seen two hundred yards or so away on the left on the west side of the road – this was used as a Battalion Headquarters for those Canadian units operating in the southerly part of the attacks on Passchendaele. **Turn right** at this junction; notice the turning on the left to which you will be returning; at this stage go on another couple of hundred yards. Before the old railway line crosses the road, on the right hand side, is the site of Seine Dug Out **[7]**, an old German pill box, where the headquarters of 44th Battalion anxiously awaited news of the situation in Decline Copse on the evening of 26th October. It was near here that the exhausted men of 20th Battalion CEF assembled on their way out of the line on the night of 11-12 November.

Return and take the road indicated (**now on your right**) and the huge cemetery of Tyne Cot will be seen just off to the left. **Proceed to Tyne Cot**. Standing by any of the bunkers in this cemetery will give you some idea of the view that the Germans had over the British lines. This is a good spot from which to see the whole of the New Zealand advance, with the exception of the northerly area beyond Gravenstafel. In particular, Peter Pan, Wolf Farm and the site of Wolf Copse may all be seen from the cemetery, situated as they are well over two kilometres away.

Having inspected the cemetery (although this may be done as a part of Walk 4), **turn right at the entrance**. The farm on your left which is reached after two hundred yards or so was known as Hamburg **[8]**. Opposite the track leading down to it, running parallel to the road on which you stand and just in the fields, was Dab Trench. This T Junction was also used as a Battalion Headquarters in the attacks of 26 and 30 October, in the first instance by 44th Battalion.

A metalled track soon after this on the right leads up to Augustus Farm **[9]** and to the north of it lies the remnants of Augustus Wood. Beyond Augustus Farm is Heine House **[10]**, inside the German lines on 30 October, which was of importance to the men of the 72nd, 27th and 20th battalions CEF. As the ground drops away below Hamburg you are going over the area over which it became impossible to attack as the battle progressed. Towards the bottom of the valley, coming from the left, was K Track, one of the duckboard tracks along which the infantry came up the line.

The road bends around sharply to the right; a few hundred yards on the right is the site of Waterfields **[11]**. The road straight ahead comes out on the Bellevue Spur, to the west of the tiny hamlet. To the left of the road, as it climbs the spur, is the site of Marsh Bottom **[12]**; on this ground New Zealand attacks foundered on 12 October. It was just to the north of Waterfields, in the vicinity of the Ravebeek, that Second Lieutenant AR Cockerell fought the action that won him the DSO.

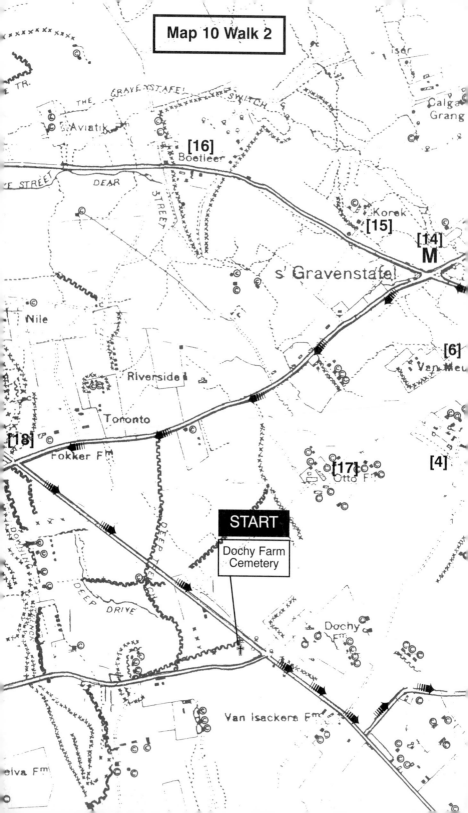

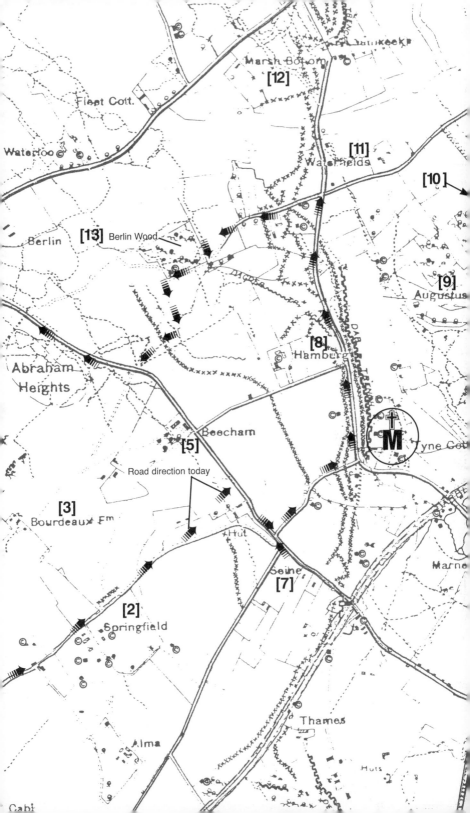

Marsh Botom
[12]

Fleet Cott.

Waterloo

[11]
Waterfields

[10]

[13] Berlin Wood

Berlin

Digob

[9]
Augustus

[8]
Hamburg

Abraham
Heights

Beecham

[5]

Road direction today

[3]

Bourdeaux Fm

Hut

Seine
[7]

Tyne Cot

Marne

[2]
Springfield

Thames

Alma

Huts

Cabl

BEECHAM FARM   GRAVENSTAFEL   HAMBURG FARM

Tyne Cot.

The New Zealanders had their start line in this area, running almost directly north to the Bellevue Road. Behind was the 3rd Australian Division which also had the road on the left (and Waterfields) within its boundary.

(At this point, **if in a car**, turn around and **retrace the route** back to **Beecham Farm**, and rejoin the tour where the track from Berlin Wood **[13]** connects with this road)

Turn left along a well defined track **towards Berlin Wood** (sometimes known as Berlin Copse), about five hundred yards distance. The Germans had pill-boxes in it, but these caused few problems to 3/Auckland and 3/Canterbury, and they were able to dig in just to the east of it. **Follow the track around the eastern and southern sides** of the wood – do not go into it as it is private property and there is nothing surviving from the war in any case. At the western edge of the wood **follow the track south** until after a couple of hundred yards it forks; take the **right hand** (or western) fork and this will bring you out on the Gravfenstafel-Broodseinde Road. At the **T Junction** with the road, look left and you will see Beecham. Immediately in front of you is the feature known as Abraham Heights, which was given its name by the Canadians in 1915. **Turn right** in the direction of Gravenstafel and look right. Note the clear views across to the Passchendaele Ridge. Consider how uncomfortable the British position would have been in the winter of 1917 if the offensive had come to a halt at the end of the fighting on 4 October; and how difficult it would have been to launch an offensive from that position in the Spring of 1918, at the beginning of the new campaigning season.

After about three hundred yards you will see a track on your left leading down to Boethoek. Beyond it, another hundred and fifty yards or so, along the road on the left is Van Meulen Farm **[6]** where 3/Otago captured a machine gun and fifty prisoners.

Continue **across the junction**, leaving the New Zealand Memorial on your right **[14]**. Immediately beyond it and to the right was a small hamlet known as Korek. Just where a track goes off to the right was a German pill-box **[15]**, possibly the one recorded in the Wellington history which caught fire. This area is well described in the chapter on the Germans at Passchendaele. The farm along the road on the right about three hundred yards beyond this track junction was Boetleer **[16]** with Hill 32 just to its south; there were German pill-boxes north and south of the road here. The New Zealanders had overrun the Wilhelm Stellung, which ran to the east of the road coming north west out of Kansas Cross and then overran the Mittel Riegel, a switch line that connected the Wilhelm Line to the Flanders I position.

Return to Gravenstafel and turn right towards Kansas Cross. After about a hundred yards or so, on your right, you will find a bunker dug in to the side of the road. Some fifteen hundred yards further on look into the fields on your left – about five hundred yards away, towards the bottom of the valley, is the site of Otto Farm **[17]** whose nest of pill boxes proved far less troublesome than had been anticipated; it was about a hundred-and-fifty yards to the northwest of a farm building.

At Kansas Cross **[18] turn left** and return to your car.

Walk 3. The Canadian Attack – North

For this walk allow about two-and-a-half to three hours.
[This walk may be done in a car]

The car should be parked at **Passchendaele New British Cemetery [1]**.

The opportunity should be taken to visit the cemetery. There are quite good views, half way down, to the northern part of the battlefield, in particular to such points as Valour **[4]** and Virile **[5]** Farms, Vine **[11]** and Vat **[6]** Cottages and Vapour **[9]** Farm; several of these places combine to form the scattered hamlet of Goudberg. Poelcappelle Church may be seen in the distance, to the north west, about two-and-a-half miles away. From this vantage point it should also be clear how difficult it was for the troops to advance on the northern side of this spur, with the ground completely open and very boggy.

Returning to the cemetery entrance, **turn right**. However, take the trouble to look across to the other side of the road: the northern part of Passchendaele is quite clear, the church, Crest Farm (an old shack on its northern side helps to identify this), Berlin Wood and the road down the Bellevue Spur. The Germans in this position (which fell relatively cheaply towards the end of the battle) had a grandstand view over the heads of their comrades as the British and Canadians advanced.

After walking about half a kilometre a **turning off downhill to the half right** will be seen; **take this**, but note the high embankment on your left **[2]**. It was on the slope of this hill that the stubborn German defenders caused so many problems to the Canadians, and in particular the PPCLI. It was in the action to remove this obstacle to their attack that MacKenzie and Mullin won their VCs.

After some three hundred yards on this new road there is a large farm on the left. Quite often, and especially in the spring and the autumn, after the ploughing, there will be found a variety of shells on the forecourt awaiting collection by the Belgian bomb squad based in Houthulst Forest. This is Furst Farm **[3]**, and it was in the vicinity of this farm that Private Kinross won his VC.

At Furst Farm look to the right. There are some stands of trees that approximate to Woodland Plantation, that ground which was, on 30 October, quite impassable. To the rear of this is Source Farm **[8]** and behind it the much larger Tournant Farm **[7]**. East of Source Farm is Vapour Farm **[9]** and Vanity House **[10]**, whilst to the south east of the latter is Vine Cottage, where Corporal Barron won his VC on 6 November.

Continue along the road and at the **junction turn right**; the left leads to Bellevue and the very heavy fighting that took place there on 26 October. The road onto which you have now turned was just behind the Flanders I line and there were numerous pill-boxes on either side of the road.

Proceeding along this road, there are good views to the east and the ground over which various Canadian and British attacks took place in the latter days of October and in early November. After a kilometre or so, **turn left**. From here and to the north the Flanders I Line was particularly strong in pill-boxes and wire, and it cost the 63rd (Naval) Division considerable casualties to try and get forward at all.

125

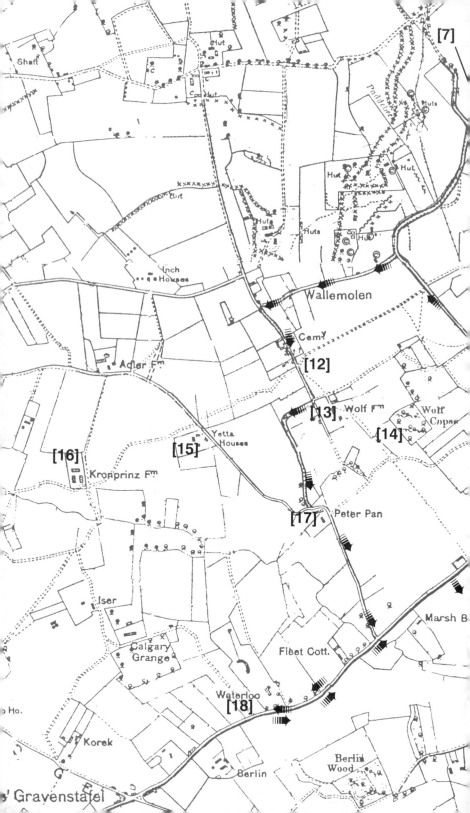

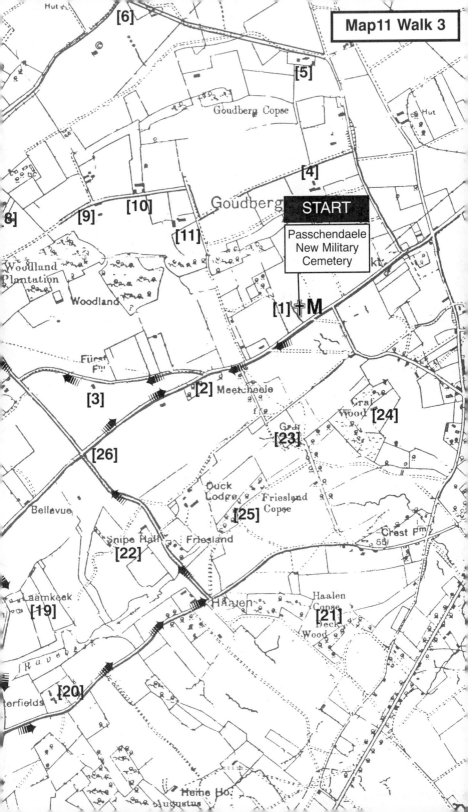

A reminder of the nature of the terrain in 1917 (26 September).

At the **T Junction** (in the village of Wallemolen) **turn left**; opposite a farm on the right hand side of the road reached after a few hundred yards is the site of the cemetery. It was captured by men of the New Zealand Rifle Brigade on 12 October, one of the very few successes of that day.

Beyond it, as the road bends to the right, is Wolf Farm **[13]**, on the left hand side of the road; it was to the north side of this that men of 2/NZRB went to find shelter from the German machine gunners on Bellevue Spur, some 1200 yards away to the south east.

About two hundred yards to the south east of Wolf Farm was Wolf Copse **[14]**; it was at the north east edge of the copse that Private Thomas Holmes of 4/CMR won his VC on 26 October.

The road turns sharply west for a short while; before turning to the south again Yetta Houses **[15]** may be seen about four hundred yards away; five hundred yards to the west of that is Kronprinz Farm **[16]**, captured by the New Zealanders on 4 October and the scene of so much distress as a battalion headquarters and dressing station during the abortive attack of 12 October.

The road drops down to Peter Pan **[17]**, snuggled away in folds in the ground just to the east of the Ravebeek. The German account of Passchendaele chapter graphically describes the conditions in this vicinity on 4 October. It was from here that the attacks of 12 and 26 October were launched.

At the Bellevue road **turn right** and walk for three hundred yards or so, passing on your right a calvary. Next to it is a large farm complex – this is on the site of Waterloo **[18]**; the fighting of 4 October here is described in the German chapter and that describing the events of 4 October. The tragic events that took place in the ground around about here and the terrible problems of getting the wounded away after the attacks of 9 and 12 October are described in the chapter on that day. It is a good position from which to examine the southern attack on Passchendaele: Berlin Wood, Tyne Cot and Passchendaele itself are all quite clear.

Retrace your steps past the turning to Peter Pan and begin the climb up the Bellevue Spur. On your right is the feature known as Marsh Bottom. Take the **first turning right**; the farmhouse on your right, reached after a hundred and fifty yards or so, was Laamkeek **[19]**. The New Zealanders had a most difficult time trying to make any progress at all here on 12 October. At the bottom of this road **turn left**. Waterfields **[20]** was opposite the farm and was inclusive to 10 (Australian) Brigade for the attack. It was just to the north of this, along the bank of the Ravebeek, that Second Lieutenant Cockerell had his extraordinary experiences on that bloody day.

Continue along this road and **take the next left turn**. Before doing this look to your right; the trees there are approximately on the site of Haalen Copse **[21]**. It was the condition of the ground there that came as such a nasty shock to the 72nd Battalion CEF on the night of 29 October. **Go up** the Bellevue Spur. On your right is Friesland **[25]** and beyond that Graf Farm **[23]** and Graf Copse **[24]**, positions from which the German defenders remained a thorn in the side of the Canadian attackers of Passchendaele right up to 6 November. Towards the top of the road, on the left, is Snipe Hall **[22]**; this was not captured on 26 October and it had to be removed before the 30 October attack could take place by a special, prior, company attack by the PPCLI. On the other side of the road, about a hundred yards distance, is the site of Duck Lodge; there is no building on or near the place where it used to be, and even the track that was there is no more.

The road junction is Bellevue **[26]**, and it was here that Shankland and Kelly won their VCs on 26 October. The chapter on the German defenders at Passchendaele gives an eloquent description of the scene here on 4 October. This crossroads area was particularly strongly defended, with thick wire and concrete fortifications on the west side of the road north and south of the Gravenstafel - Mosselmarkt road.

Turn right here and make your way to the car, remembering to look out for the site of the pill-box at Meetcheele, about fifty yards south west of the turning down to Furst Farm.

Walk 4. The Canadian Attack – South

The first part of this tour has to be walked; however the tour can be abbreviated and the rest done by car should it be desirable or necessary.

The car should be parked at Tyne Cot Cemetery. Please be warned to ensure that you lock up valuables in the boot or, better still, take them with you. Although not as prone to theft from cars as the Somme was a year or two ago, it makes perfect sense to take usual precautions and remove temptation.

Do not visit the cemetery at this point. **Walk back towards the old railway line** and towards the main Broodseinde - Passchendaele road. The course of the old railway line where it crosses the road is quite apparent. This was known as Dash Crossing **[2]**. There is a road that runs parallel and to the west of the railway; do not go along this, but about a hundred yards along here and on the road's west side was the local cemetery, Keerselaarhoek Cemetery.

You should **proceed along the line of the old railway** which is now a walking/cycle lane. It can get quite muddy along here, but not too boggy. Quite often the line is in a cutting. It crosses the main road at Defy Crossing **[16]**; after about a hundred yards you are crossing the old 26 October British Front Line. The line goes through another cutting

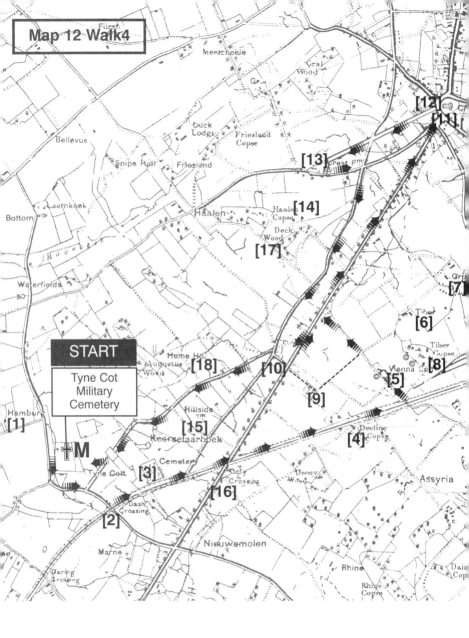

and becomes quite wooded on either side – this is the area of Decline Copse **[4]** which is of such importance to the 44th, 46th and 85th battalions CEF: the two chapters on the Canadians on the 26 and 30 October should be read in conjunction with this part of the walk.

When the line emerges at a **road crossing**, **turn left** on to the road. Soon you will come to Vienna Cott **[5]** on your right; in the middle distance may be seen Tiber **[6]** and Grun **[7]**, with Tiber Copse **[8]** just to the south west of Tiber and about fifty or so yards to the east of Vienna. **Walk on about a hundred-and-fifty yards**. In the fields on your left, about two hundred yards away, you should see a small, cenotaph type memorial. This is the 85th (Nova Scotia Highlanders) Battalion CEF memorial **[9]**. It should be possible to gain access to the memorial along the field line here. If that does not seem practicable, continue on the road and then **turn left at the junction**; after a short walk a lawn path will appear on your left which leads up to the memorial. It marks, almost, the limit of the Canadian advance in this area – in fact the 85th had a command post here whilst the men carried on operations against Vienna, Tiber and Grun.

It is a spot where for the first time, perhaps, one can appreciate the difference it made holding this position rather than one five hundred yards or so west. The view over the German positions is considerable, and they no longer had ground views over the Salient – or at least to nothing like the same extent.

Follow the grass path to the main road. Opposite you will see a large red and white mast **[10]** – a very useful indicator for position on the ridge. Those who wish to return to their cars at this point should **cross the road go down a minor road**, **turn left** and at the **fork turn right** – this will bring you to the **back of Tyne Cot** which you may enter from the memorial end – this would be a good time to visit the cemetery,

The more stalwart should **turn right on reaching the road** and soon they will pass the sign proclaiming Passendaele (British and German, Passchendaele). Besides its fame as a World War One battle site the village does produce an excellent, albeit pricey, cheese.

It is quite a long walk into the centre; the village does boast some cafes, a bakery and some eating places – I recommend that you get addresses and opening hours from the tourist office at Zonnebeke. The Church is generally open, and the very fine 66th Division memorial window is in the north aisle chapel. In the market square is one of a series of, occasionally, rather misleading Australian War memorials of recent (early 90s) vintage, in the form of a relief map and an explanation. The town hall is away off to the right from this; on the walls may be found a series of plaques, described in the Memorials section, to various liberators and defenders of this place **[13]**.

Having taken refreshment of some sort, now **proceed to** the **Canadian Memorial** at Crest Farm **[13]**. It was in the vicinity of this approach road that Private Robertson won his posthumous VC in the capture of the village on 6 November 1917.

Crest Farm Memorial is no longer as well sited as once it was – the problem being that the village has extended westwards and obscures some of the dominant views that this knoll had over the two spurs coming off the ridge. But still something of the strength of the position may be perceived if you go to the **western side** of the memorial and look across to Bellevue and Graf Farm.

Return towards Passchendaele but take the **right hand road** and then take the **first right**. This new road was the right hand boundary of the 72nds. As you leave Passchendaele, on your right, is the site of Deck Wood **[17]**. In due course the road comes to a junction with a road going off to the left – this will bring you out opposite the 85th Battalion memorial. Where the **road forks**, take the **right hand fork** and over on your right you will see Heine House **[18]**. There were various dug out outpost positions a hundred yards or so away from it, used by the attacking battalions on 30 October and 6 and 10 November. When you pass a farmhouse close to the road on the right on the left you will see Hillside Farm **[15]** (sometimes House) which was used for a variety of purposes by the Canadians, including an aid post on the night of 26 October. There are good views over to the right, to positions such as Augustus and Hamburg Farm **[1]** as well as to Berlin Wood, well off to the north west.

Soon you will come to the walls of the Memorial at Tyne Cot; it is possible to enter the

Tyne Cot in 1920 – the battle ground is beginning to recover from its ordeal.

ground of the Memorial and cemetery from here and time should be spent visiting this quite stupendous and awesome place before returning to the car.

A Car Tour 5 – The Northern Part of the Battlefield

This quite short car tour is to enable the visitor to view some of the most northerly parts of the ground crossed by units in their attempt to secure the Passchendaele Ridge.

The start point for this tour is Kansas Cross **[1]**; head in a north westerly direction towards Langemarck. The large farm on the left, seen after about five hundred yards, is

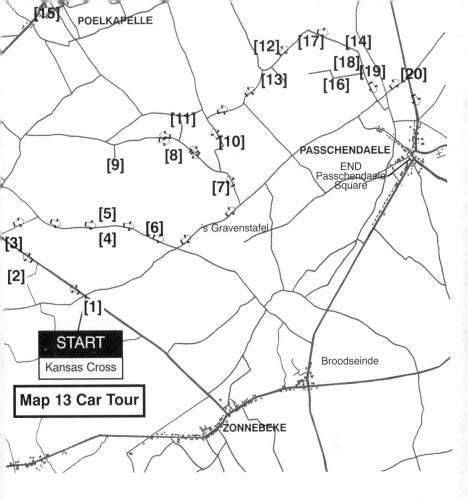

Schuler Farm **[2]**, scene of many incidents during the war; the line ran through here on 20 September. Take the **next turning right** (the farm on the corner is Winnipeg **[3]**) and then take the **right at the T Junction**. After a kilometre or so, Boetleer **[5]** will be on your left and Hill 32 **[4]** on your left, the scene of heavy fighting on 4 October. The New Zealand Division captured most of the ground that you can see in that area, up to and beyond Kronprinz Farm.

Further on is the Korek position **[6]** (on the left); the New Zealanders suffered heavy casualties coming up from the valley of the Hannebeek. At the memorial, **turn left**, towards Mosselmarkt. Take the **turning for Peter Pan [7]**, passing Waterloo on the way. At Peter Pan take the **left hand fork**; after a few hundred yards you will see Yetta Houses **[8]** on your left. After another three to four hundred yards you will see the track leading down to Kronprinz Farm, a key German position on 4 October and the scene of human tragedy and misery on 9 and 12 October.

Turn around here, but note the view to the north west the tower of Langemarck and almost due north that of Poelcappelle **[15]**. This is the ground over which the British divisions alongside the Dominion divisions had to fight.

133

Return to Peter Pan and turn left, going north past Wolf Farm **[10]**; **turn right** in Wallemolen and then after several hundred yards **turn left at the T Junction**. The road carries you over the Paddebeek; at the junction turn right. The farm now on your left is close to the site of Tournant Farm **[12]** ; on your right, down in the valley is Source Farm **[13]**; from here eastwards is where Major Pearkes saved the situation on 30 October and won his VC.

Proceed along this road until you come to a turning to the half right; the building on your right is Vat Cottages **[17]**. Stop at a convenient point and look to your right and down into the valley. Almost directly south, about eight hundred yards away, is where Corporal Barron got his VC at Vine Cottage **[16]** on 6 November.

This area is known as Goudberg **[14]**. Follow the road until you come to **a junction** where you will **turn right**; on your right is Virile Farm **[18]** and at the next turning on the right there is a farm that is close to the site of Valour Farm **[19]**. Continue on the original road until the Gravenstafel road and **turn left**. The cross roads that is soon reached was known as Vindictive Cross Roads **[20]**. **Turn right** and stop the car as soon as may be practicable. The Canadian line extended about two hundred yards to the north of this point and formed a notable salient. The high point of the Westrosebeke Ridge is in that vicinity, and by crossing the road the tower of the village church may be seen – actually to best advantage in the middle of the raod, but there are obvious hazards about this on such a busy route!

This was where the great battle that had commenced on 31 July ended.

Return to your car and drive in to the square in Passchendaele and seek liquid refreshment.

Visiting the battlefield at Passchendaele can best be done in the late autumn and the spring, when the fields are clear and leaves do not obstruct views. However, the obvious downside is the weather and the quite common poor visibility. Although little remains to show the physical scars of what took place here eighty years ago, enough exists, and the landscape so unchanged, that one can get a better understanding of what happened, even if there is no possibility of us being able to understand what it was that all those who fought in this campaign endured and suffered.

Passchendaele: The Cemeteries

The area around Passchendaele has comparatively few British cemeteries compared to many other parts of the Ypres Salient. There are a number of reasons for this. The battle for Passchendaele Ridge was in the main fought over the period of late September to mid November 1917. The position was precarious and the line was lost in the spring of 1918, giving the British little time or security to deal with the dead scattered around the battlefield. Survival of the living was the order of the day. The Germans did relatively little to 'tidy up' the battlefield when the new line stabilised considerably closer to Ypres, and they in due turn were ejected after a short battle in September 1918.

The nature of the ground during the latter phase of Third Ypres was such that even if there had been the manpower and willingness to take the dead to the rear and bury them, the practicalities made this almost impossible. Many dead were shoved into one of the innumerable shell holes in the hope that they might be recovered later. The continuing heavy fighting in the vicinity meant that many of the recorded, isolated burial places of individuals were simply destroyed in the later fighting or got lost as makeshift markers were moved or disappeared in the hurly-burly of activities and movement in the battlefield. Many were simply lost to the mud.

The cemeteries below Passchendaele and Broodseinde ridges are generally large concentration cemeteries; the small one at Polygon Wood, opposite Buttes New Cemetery, is a unique exception.

There are, therefore, fewer cemeteries in this guide to be visited than is usual; I have confined myself to four. The Commonwealth War Graves Commission continues to provide these with registers, despite their persistent theft by a number of selfish, and quite possibly stupid, individuals. As explained elsewhere in this book, it is possible to find out details of individual casualties that might be of interest to the visitor from the Commission, and there is an office in Ypres open at normal working hours where details may also be obtained.

BRIDGE HOUSE CEMETERY

This is one of the smallest cemeteries in the Salient, with only forty five burials. Unusually only four of these are unknown, and nearly all the burials are from the last few days of September 1917, associated with the Battle of Polygon Wood which was fought between 26 September and 3 October. The exception is Private W Baker [C. 1] of 14/Royal Irish Rifles; he was a casualty on 16 August 1917, during the Battle of Langemarck when his battalion lost many men in front of Pond Farm, further up the road. The casualties from the 1/7th King's Liverpool were victims of the attack by their division, the 55th, on 20th September.

The remainder were members of the 59th (North Midland) Division, consisting of second line battalions of Territorial regiments. There are a few members of their attached medical and engineer units buried here as well.

Bridge House was part of the German Second Line position and was captured by the evening of 31 July 1917. It was used regularly subsequently as a dressing station by a number of units, but the 59th were the only ones to establish it as a cemetery, possibly because of their situation during the battle. Rather more remarkable is that the graves should have survived, given the terrific pasting that the road from Wieltje was given in subsequent artillery and bombing operations by the Germans.

It is an unusual and peaceful cemetery, hard by the new Bridge House Farm, and in a relatively quiet part of the Salient. Should there be no register here, this cemetery also appears in the registers that should be found at Dochy Farm New British Cemetery and Seaforth Cemetery, Cheddar Villa.

DOCHY FARM NEW BRITISH CEMETERY

The farm after which this cemetery was named was off to the east, on the other side of the road, from the location of today's cemetery.

This is a concentration cemetery, and had no existence prior to the end of the war. It is unusual in both this respect and in the fact that the bodies that were brought in were all isolated graves – ie there is no concentration here of small graveyards. I have found this a point for reflection as I have walked along its rows – all of these men had, in all probability, been left where they fell during the battle, or perhaps were pushed into a shell hole and perfunctorily marked with a rifle stabbed in the ground, if they were lucky. The reason for the cemetery is also indicated by its location – along a road that was maintained in some form throughout the war, in the middle of a battle zone, with other connecting routes to parts of the battlefield nearby and with a (wartime) light railway almost alongside. This made it a central point to bring in the bodies from the battlefields around Boesinghe, St Julien, Frezenburg and Passchendaele.

There are almost 1,450 men buried in this cemetery; two thirds of them (958) are unidentified. This alone bears witness to the haphazard way in which so many were buried during Third Ypres; or to the ferocity of the artillery duel that took place over the ground. The cemetery has representatives from almost all corners of the Empire and Dominions, with the single (and understandable) exception of India, as only Indian cavalry remained on the Western Front at this time. The solitary Newfoundlander, Private Aaron Douglas, was killed on 29 September 1918 [III B 18]. His battalion had recently, on the 13th of that month, been transferred to the 9th (Scottish) Division, and he was killed in the final breakout from the Salient. His division was attacking Broodseinde Ridge, and it seems appropriate that at least one representative of that surge from the hitherto all-encompassing Salient should find his resting place amongst those who had striven so hard for a similar objective the previous year. Although the British West Indies Regiment has none of its members here, the 19 year old Private AL Browne of the PWO Civil Service Rifles had his home in Barbados [VI C 20]. Perhaps the most unusual entry is that of Private M Goldstein of 2/Middlesex [VII A 1]. Although his parents lived in London, he is recorded as being a 'native of Russia'. He was one of the thirty four members of his battalion killed or missing during the attack of 16 August 1917.

The cemetery gives extensive views across to the east, with Passchendaele and Tyne Cot being visible in clear weather.

PASSCHENDAELE NEW BRITISH CEMETERY

This was another concentration cemetery created after the Armistice, and is also composed of isolated graves, in this case found from the battlefields of Passchendaele and Langemarck. The cemetery has panoramic views over to the flatter ground to the north and the more undulating terrain to the south, whilst to the west the flat ground on which it stands on top of the Bellevue spur obscures that outlook.

An inspection of the register shows the large numbers of Canadians and Australians (in particular) who were first generation immigrants to their respective countries; this probably helps to explain why these Dominions were able to raise such substantial bodies of men by voluntary means. The PPCLI, when it was first raised at the outbreak of the war, was able to claim a veteran of every regiment in the British Army, except one, within its ranks.

Private Oscar Abramson of the 20th Canadian Infantry, had his origins, however, in Riga, Latvia [XII E 26]. Second Lieutenant S Crowther of 29th Squadron RFC, a fighter pilot from Toronto, seems to have been the only pilot casualty over this part of the front during the first day of the Battle of the Menin Road on 20 September [VII E 30]. The Reverend Harry Dickinson was killed on 30 October whilst serving with the Artists

Rifles, then part of 63rd (Naval) Division. He is commemorated amongst the Special memorials at the rear of the cemetery; he is believed to be among those buried here. His battalion launched an attack on Source Trench, some four hundred yards to the west of Source Farm, to the north west of the cemetery, and got hit by close range machine guns and were left floundering in the mud. A Roman Catholic Chaplain in a fellow brigade had been badly wounded in the division's last big battle, a few days earlier.

Private Alexander Decoteau was an Indian from the Red Pheasant Reserve in Saskatchewan; he was killed on 30 October by a sniper [XI A 28]. In August 1985 a colourful ceremony was held by his tribe to lay his spirit to rest, 'believing that without an Indian burial [his] spirit was left to wander the earth'.[1]

Lieutenant David Gunn was a member of the Seaforth Highlanders who was killed on 13 October [XVI C 21]. Although his parents had moved to South London it is clear that their Highland loyalties remained; their house's name was 'Seaforth'. Captain Rider Haggard of the PPCLI had a famous literary uncle, Sir Henry Rider Haggard, the author of, amongst other books, King Solomon's Mines. Captain Haggard enlisted as a private in the regiment in 1914, one of the first to enlist. He was commissioned in 1915 and commanded a company at Courcelette on the Somme, in 1916 and at Vimy in the April of 1917 [VIII A 19].

Amongst the Canadians there were a fair number of citizens of the United States – for example Private McQuaid of Buffalo, New York [IX A 27] and Private George Kline of Roxbury, Massachusetts [XIII B 25]. On the American entry into the war there was no great move to get these men into the United States Army; in 1915 the British and the French had come to an arrangement whereby their citizens serving in the other's army were returned to their national force.

A most unusual entry is that of Lance Corporal A Payne, MM [X E 29]. Whilst there is nothing particularly unusual about him, he was married to a French lady who had not remarried by the time the registers were compiled (this one, like many others, was printed in 1928). He met her in all probability whilst serving at the front, for her home address is given as Fleurbaix, a village in the British line below Aubers Ridge.

There are a fair number of members of the 85th Battalion (Nova Scotia Regiment) buried in this cemetery. Reference to their battalion memorial, unique on this battlefield, is made elsewhere in this guide.

At the introduction to the register it is stated that almost all of the casualties are from the autumn of 1917. There are quite a few from the days of holding the line during the long winter of 1917-1918, but the register states that, 'one is identified who fell in November 1914 and one other who fell in May 1915'. I had quite a careful look but could not find the November 1914 casualty (quite likely, given the battle raging in the Salient at that time).

Private George Mason was killed whilst serving with 2/Cheshires on 5 May 1915 [XIII E 1]. It is quite probable that he was killed during the withdrawal of the battalion to Frezenburg, towards the end of the Battle of St Julien, during the Second Battle of Ypres when the Germans first made extensive use of gas. The battalion had been holding a position along the Gravenstafel-Wieltje Road. It is likely that his date of death is incorrect and probably refers to the date on which it was reported – the battalion had moved away from this position on 4 May.

Rather more mysterious is the presence in the cemetery of Lieutenant Whitford Weston, 3rd Battalion Canadian Infantry [XIV F 19]; although he was killed on 13 June 1916, the register does not include him among the non-1917 and 1918 casualties. He was a casualty of the German attack, mainly on the Canadians, in the Battle of Mount Sorrel, a battle which lasted from 2 - 13 June 1916. This battle took place entirely in the area between Hooge and Mount Sorrel and therefore his presence here, in a cemetery some miles away, is a mystery. Perhaps he died of wounds in German captivity or he was hit by a shell and buried hastily by his captors en route to the rear.

This is a quiet and surprisingly unvisited cemetery; built on the slope of the ridge its position provides a suitably reflective place to consider the great battle for Passchendaele and in this respect is preferable to the much visited Tyne Cot cemetery.

TYNE COT CEMETERY AND MEMORIAL

It should be noted that the register for the cemetery is at the entrance; that of the memorial is kept in its left (northern) hand pavilion.

This cemetery is an awesome sight, of the same visual impact as the American and many of the German and French cemeteries. There are row after row of white headstones, stretching up towards the walls of the memorial that provide the rear wall of this, the largest British cemetery in the world. When I first came on a visit to the Salient with my father in the summer of 1968 it would seem likely that we were the only visitors to the cemetery that day. Now it is almost impossible to find a day from the spring to the late autumn when there is not someone else – quite often a coachload of people – in the cemetery at the same time. This is, of course, a tremendously heartening development, as it shows a considerable revival in interest in the Great War and means that eighty years on there is continuing homage paid to those who gave their lives. On the other hand the cemetery's fabric, most notably the lawns, has suffered considerably from the tramping of hundreds of feet. The cemetery, by the nature of its scale, does not have the same reflective atmosphere provided by so many of the smaller, less visited British cemeteries; some argue that this is no bad thing, that the garden cemeteries anaesthetise the senses and diminish the horror and carnage that characterises war.

The original cemetery was centred on the largest of the remaining three pill-boxes within the cemetery grounds. After the cemetery was captured by 3rd Australian Division (not the 2nd, as stated in the register) this pill-box became an Advanced Dressing Station for several divisions, and thus the cemetery sprang up. It is said that George Vth, on his pilgrimage to the Battlefields after the war in 1922, was most keen that these original burials should not be reinterred when the cemetery was expanded, but should be left where they were to indicate something of the origins of the burial ground. These original graves number a few hundred, a number of them effectively small mass graves, with several soldiers commemorated under one or two headstones; there are also a few German burials in these plots [I and II, to the east and south of the pill-box].

The cross of sacrifice, on the suggestion of the King, is mounted on top of this bunker, and the views from it across the length and breadth of the Salient are tremendous. It clearly shows the achievement of the attacking troops in gaining this ground, yet the memorial wall obscures the achievement of the army in capturing the higher ground to the east – attacks which lasted several weeks after this ground was captured on 6th October.

After the war the army spent three years scouring the battlefield for bodies, and they were brought here from all parts of the Salient, generally from north of the Menin Road, with the bulk coming from the ground around Zonnebeke, below and around Passchendaele, and around Langemarck and Poelcapelle. Also a number of smaller cemeteries were concentrated here from the Salient and further afield; in one or two cases the cemeteries were destroyed in later fighting; for example Zonnebeke British Cemetery No 2 was created by the Germans in April 1915 and many of those buried there are commemorated by Special Memorials along the wall to the left of the cemetery entrance.

Soldiers here represent all parts of the war, from October 1914 to September 1918,

138

when the war finally moved on and peace once more returned to this agricultural region of Belgium. In this section I have confined myself generally to those who fell in the battle covered by this book; others will be detailed in later works.

One of those killed towards the end of the war, CSM C Attrill of 2/Hants [LIV F 15] seemed only to have a mother in law left to remember him. Private Douglas Cole-Baker MM [IV D 7] was born in Tipperary, but his parents noted that their 28 year old son had been a 'landowner in New Zealand for ten years'. Second Lieutenant George Cowie was only aged 18 when he was killed on 22 October flying a Sopwith Pup [I AA 21]; his is one of the original burials. Lieutenant Guy Drummond, was killed at Second Ypres on 22 April 1915; his father was Sir George Drummond, a Canadian politician, president of the Bank of Montreal and largely responsible for the deepening of the ship canal between Montreal and Quebec. He was one of several children, in this case of Sir George's second wife. Second Lieutenant Wilfred Goulden was killed on 12 February 1918 whilst his battalion, 2/Middx, was on the Bellevue spur [XX A 9]. He was the battalion Intelligence Officer. CQMS Sidney Jones [XI C 3] must have considered himself fortunate not to have been given his father's name, Caesar Augustus.

Brigadier-General James Riddell [[XXXIV H 14] was killed whilst commanding 1st/1st Northumberland Infantry Brigade (149 Brigade, 50th (Northumbrian) Division) during Second Ypres on 26 April 1915. He was killed as he went forward to make contact with his battalion commanders about 150 yards south of Vanheule Farm, south of St Julian.2 His brigade had only arrived in France five days earlier. One of his successors, Brigadier-General H Clifford, was killed by a sniper before High Wood. Captain Vivian Hugh Nicholas, 1/Hants and RFC was killed in action whilst flying over the German lines on 17 January 1916 [LXII C 5]. He was one of thirty four pilots who flew from Salisbury Plain to France on 12 August 1914.

There are three holders of the Victoria Cross in the cemetery, as well as several commemorated on the walls of the memorial. Two of the former are Australians – Captain C Jeffries [XL E 1] and Sergeant L McGee [XX D 1]. Private J Robertson's VC is covered elsewhere in this book [LVIII D 26]. The citations for these VC winners may be found in the register for the cemetery at the entrance.

THE TYNE COT MEMORIAL TO THE MISSING

The graceful wall which encompasses the eastern side of the cemetery has on it the names of just under thirty five thousand men with no known grave. When it became clear that the Menin gate Memorial in Ypres was not going to be big enough to take all the names of the missing in the Salient, it was determined to use this site for those killed after (approximately) August 5 1917.

The names are by Regiment in order of Army precedence. However the missing from almost all of the Dominion Armies are recorded on the Menin Gate and not here. The exception is New Zealand; the central apse here has the names of their missing on this battlefield, almost 1,200 of them. This follows national practice; New Zealand's memorials to the missing are located as closely as possible to the battlefield where they were lost. Thus there is a beautiful memorial in Buttes New British Cemetery in Polygon Wood, on Messines Ridge and in Caterpillar Valley Cemetery on the Somme.

The memorial is fourteen foot high and five hundred foot long. The seemingly endless lists of names are a mute but effective reminder of the cost of war.

1 Daniel Dancocks, *Legacy of Valour*, p 149
2 Frank Davies and Graham Maddocks, *Bloody Red Tabs* p 101-102

Memorials and Bunkers

NEW ZEALAND MEMORIAL AT S GRAVENSTAFEL
This fine memorial stands near a crossroads, to the north of the road running from Wieltje to Passchendaele. It commemorates the part played by New Zealand in the Battle of Broodseinde, 4 October 1917. There is a similar one at Messines and another between Longueval and Flers on the Somme. The common feature on all of them is the legend 'From the furthest corners of the earth'. The New Zealand Memorials to the missing are found in the nearest big cemetery to the action – thus in the case of Third Ypres at Tyne Cot and Buttes cemetery, Polygon Wood. The New Zealand government made a conscious decision that none of the gravestones would have personal messages from their relations carved at the bottom, as is usual. Unfortunately, because of the trees and the nearby buildings, this is not a particularly good viewing spot.

On the road heading west, back towards Ypres, there is a well preserved bunker on the right-hand-side of the road.

ALBERTINA MEMORIAL, PASSCHENDAELE NEW MILITARY CEMETERY
This is one of a series of memorials which was erected in the early 80s to commemorate the final battle in the area, when an Anglo-Belgian army under the King of the Belgians finally pushed toe Germans off the ridge surrounding Ypres. This battle commenced on 28 September.

PASSCHENDAELE TOWN HALL WALL
There are a variety of commemorative tablets erected on the Town Hall wall facing the square. The most noticeable, but also most recent, is A Western Front Association plaque erected in September 1988 to commemorate the fact that there had been a battle at all; until this time there was no memorial to the Third Battle of Ypres. Other plaques are to the Belgian regiments who liberated the village in September 1918; to those who defended it in May 1940; and to the Poles (the Polish Armoured Division) who liberated it in September1944.

PASSCHENDAELE PARISH CHURCH
In the north window in a side chapel is a magnificent stained glass window which is the Divisional memorial of the 66th (2/East Lancs) Division. This division arrived in France in March 1917 and fought its first big action here, suffering heavy casualties on 9 October. It was reduced to cadre strength after heavy losses in the German spring offensive, but took its part in the Advance to Victory in the last six or seven weeks of the war when it was commanded by Major-General HK Bethell, remarkable as being the youngest divisional commander of either war and for having the most volcanic and unreasonable temper.

CREST FARM
This is the farm that was captured by the 72nd Battalion CEF on 30 October. The development of the village on the south side rather detracts from the views that this commanding position gave to the German defenders of Passchendaele. It is one of a series of simple memorials that stretch all along the Western Front where the Canadians fought significant actions

85TH BATTALION MEMORIAL
This memorial is more fully described in the chapter on the attack of 30 October. It was erected by the battalion before it returned to Canada at the end of the war. On leaving Passchendaele, on the right-hand-side, a red and white radio mast may be observed; the memorial is about a hundred yards into the field on the opposite side of the road. Although it is difficult to park, do not be tempted to stop on the road. The grass verge on the memorial side of the road is usually dry and wide enough to take a car.

TYNE COT BUNKERS

Within the cemetery there are three bunkers, and the remnants of another one in private property to the east of it. They formed a German strongpoint around farm buildings which were known as Tyne Cot (Tyneside Cottages), thus named by the 50th (Northumbrian) Division. It is the largest group of bunkers remaining in the area and is useful in indicating something of the cluster system of pill-boxes that the Germans used so successfully in their defence of the ridge.

THE BREMEN REDOUBT (Not on maps provided)

This huge bunker, part of a German defence line, was uncovered in the early 1980s inside the Zonnebeke Brick Factory, which is easily identified by its set of three huge chimney stacks. It is situated at the rear of the brickyard and access is possible, usually via the Zonnebeke Tourist Office. It gives an atmospheric idea of what it must have been like to live in such cramped, if secure conditions, although it is lacking the terrifying aspects of concussion, stench and rats.

Further Reading

Although there is quite a body of literature on Passchendaele it pales into insignificance beside that written about the Somme.

The Road to Passchendaele, John Terraine, is a source book which provides selected documentation on all aspects of the battle with his accustomed trenchant observations.

In Flanders Field, Leon Wolff, although quite an old book (first published 1958), is still in print and highly rated by some. It had a considerable effect on opinion at the time of its publication. It is written in an easy style, but it is partisan and nearly all of the opinions expressed in it would be liable to be challenged.

They called it Passchendaele, Lyn Macdonald, is the first in her series of books that have covered the years of the war (we await 1918). It is based on numerous interviews with veterans, and using these interwoven with a narrative to tell the story of the battle. It is a readable and evocative book.

Legacy of Valour: The Canadians at Passchendaele, Daniel Dancocks, is rarely seen in this country, unfortunately. It is a narrative history, although it includes considerable criticism of Lloyd George and tends to support the Generals. The book, understandably, concentrates upon the considerable Canadian effort and spends time on the controversy involving Passchendaele (amongst other actions) and their highly successful Corps commander, Currie.

Passchendaele, the Untold Story, Robin Prior and Trevor Wilson, is the most recent academic study of the battle. It is critical of most of the military decisions made, both in the launching and in the conduct of the battle. It really does not have that much to say on the battles covered in this book.

The Third Ypres: Passchendaele, The Day by Day Account, Chris McCarthy, is, at its most basic, simply that. It lists what happened in brief form each day of the battle, including details such as the weather and VCs won. It is profusely illustrated and has plenty of quite clear trench maps. It lists British and German divisions and VCs in separate appendices. It is interesting to note that over a third of this book is devoted to the time scale covered in this guide.

Passchendaele in Perspective, the Third Battle of Ypres, ed Peter Liddle goes a long way to filling scholarly gaps about the battle and has contributions from a range of scholars from all over the world, each dealing with a particular aspect of Third Ypres.

There are, of course, various guides to the Salient. The chief among these that I would recommend is ***Before Endeavours Fade***, Rose Coombs MBE. This is a vade mecum to, chiefly, the British battlefields of the Great War and is enormously useful in finding the remnants of the war, memorials and cemeteries. This book is an essential part of any tourer's luggage. Very useful is Major and Mrs Holt's *Battle Map of the Ypres Salient*, which marks cemeteries, memorials, museums and so forth on a good scale map. There is a small guide that accompanies it, but in the near future there will be a much fuller guide book. These items may be purchased in a variety of museums and the Tourist Information Office in Ypres.

Selective Index

142